going to hell in a hen basket

also by robert alden rubin

Poetry Out Loud
On the Beaten Path: An Appalachian Pilgrimage
Love Poetry Out Loud

going to hell in a hen basket

an illustrated
dictionary
of modern
malapropisms

robert alden rubin

illustrations by the author

FLATIRON
BOOKS
NEW YORK

For Bill Harmon,

. . . oh, air, pride, plume here

Buckle!

———————

GOING TO HELL IN A HEN BASKET. Copyright © 2015 by Robert Alden Rubin. All rights reserved. Printed in the United States of America. For information, address Flatiron Books, 175 Fifth Avenue, New York, N.Y. 10010.

www.flatironbooks.com

Designed by Steven Seighman

The Library of Congress Cataloging-in-Publication Data is available upon request.

ISBN 978-1-250-06627-5 (hardcover)
ISBN 978-1-250-06628-2 (e-book)

Flatiron books may be purchased for educational, business, or promotional use. For information on bulk purchases, please contact the Macmillan Corporate and Premium Sales Department at 1-800-221-7945, extension 5442, or write to specialmarkets@macmillan.com.

First Edition: August 2015

10 9 8 7 6 5 4 3 2 1

contents

acknowledgments

The author gratefully acknowledges the work of the contributors to *Language Log* (LANGUAGELOG.LDC.UPENN.EDU), who have been discussing eggcorns and malapropisms on the Internet for more than a decade, and Chris Waigl's Internet *Eggcorn Database* (EGGCORNS.LASCRIBE.NET), which brings together many of the word lists and discussions that malaprop-hunters have compiled over the years on various blogs and Web sites. They served as an inspiration and a starting point for this book.

Thanks to my correspondents and friends who contributed to the project: Eloise Grathwohl, Lila Thompson, Paul Baerman, Margie Allen, Kim Geiger, and Beverly Goble; and to Cary and Bob Phillips for the Wacom Tablet, which made the drawing much easier. I am especially grateful to my agent, Liz Darhansoff, who liked the idea and connected me to the wordplay-loving folks at Flatiron Books; to Flatiron's editors Colin Dickerman and Jasmine Faustino; and to copyeditor Robert Ickes. All helped me turn it from idea to book.

And, finally, thanks to my wife, Catherine, for whose help and support I can never find the proper words.

introduction

which came first, the chicken or the eggcorn?

The first published account of an *eggcorn* seen in the wild appeared September 23, 2003, as a note by the linguist Mark Liberman in *Language Log*, a blog devoted to our English language and language in general. One of Liberman's correspondents had asked about a writer who used the phrase *egg corn* when *acorn* was meant. Another contributor to *Language Log*, the linguist Geoffrey Pullum, then proposed the term *eggcorn* to describe that sort of mistake.

Over the years, *Language Log* has noted many eggcorns that the linguists and their readers have spotted in the wilderness of the world and on the World Wide Web. In fact, the blog's contributors have helped create a substantial Internet database and discussion forum devoted to the identification and classification of eggcorns.

Language Log is a blog by self-professed "descriptive linguists." In other words (no pun intended, of course), they're interested in describing how language *is* used rather than in prescribing how it *should* be used. As scientists and scholars of the language, they would never tut-tut at verbal or textual flubs that violate the rules or sense of what language scolds call "proper" English. Their duty is to note, describe, and discuss said flubs.

Shakespeare made no such distinctions. One of his great comic characters, the constable Dogberry in *Much Ado About Nothing*, enforces the law but commits crimes against the language. Shakespeare leaves no doubt: Dogberry is a clever moron—we're meant to laugh at him.

One word, sir! Dogberry requests of Leonato, governor of Messina. *Our watch, sir, have indeed comprehended two aspicious persons.*

Leonato eventually figures out that Dogberry's deputies have *apprehended* two *suspicious* persons and tells him to interrogate the villains. Their arrest, like that of the Watergate burglars, marks the unraveling of a nefarious plot.

The Irish-born playwright Richard Brinsley Sheridan, writing 175 years after Shakespeare, created another memorable mangler of language in his play *The Rivals*. Her name is Mrs. Malaprop, and she is famous for the phrases *She's as headstrong as an allegory on the banks of the Nile*, and *He is the very pineapple of politeness*, among others. Indeed, Mrs. Malaprop, whose name literally means *inappropriate*, became synonymous with the kind of verbal goof that afterward became known as a *malapropism*.

Classic literary malapropisms of the sort committed by Dogberry and Mrs. Malaprop are driven by distinctions between social classes. They are uttered by characters who aspire to impress their betters—but fail by comically garbling the language. *Pineapple* sounds like *pinnacle*, and Mrs. Malaprop doesn't know the difference; the educated reader or playgoer does. The long-winded Dogberry, when told by Leonato that he is *tedious*, takes it as a compliment, replying, *If I were as tedious as a king, I could find it in my heart to bestow it all of your worship.*

Eggcorns are just malapropisms—misspellings or misuses of language that invite comic readings. But eggcorns differ from Mrs. Malaprop's sort of mistakes in several ways.

For one thing, eggcorns make some sense: An acorn (if one removes the acorn's cap) is shaped like an egg. And the nut also resembles a kernel of corn, or a seed. So if you were to hear the word *acorn* spoken unclearly, and hadn't seen it spelled out before, it would be perfectly logical to think that the egg-shaped nuts hanging from an oak tree were called *egg corns*. Eggcorns thus have a semantic logic to them, even if that logic makes perfect nonsense.

For another thing, those who employ eggcorns aren't pretending to be something they're not—they're not usually aspiring to an elite vocabulary or sophistication that will help them break through barriers of education and class, those staples of British humor. Eggcorns are quintessentially modern and democratic malapropisms: Their language is that of pop culture, cliché, pseudo-bureaucratic business boilerplate, secondhand phrases, and talk-radio blather. Those who inadvertently create them (*eggcornists? eggcorners? eggcornvicts? eggcoroners?*) aren't scrupulous writers, and when they feel inspired to write they often use phrases, words, and ideas that they haven't seen written down before—and get them wrong.

More important, they aren't really *trying* to appear literate and sophisticated; they're writing to friends who don't much care if they're *peaked* or *piqued*. Most of these malapropisms are not the work of journalists whose editors should know better, or of academic or literary authors whose mistakes should embarrass them.* They're the work of fan-fiction authors, gamers, blog commentators, tweeters, Facebook friends, and small-time Internet entrepreneurs advertising their businesses with more enthusiasm than sophistication.

Sometimes their mistakes produce new words. (*Eggcorn* itself has begun to appear in far more respectable and scientific dictionaries than this one.) But often eggcorn-creators just substitute one like-sounding word for another. For instance, a migraine sufferer wrote to the experts at

---

*NOTE: The examples that this book has harvested from the Web are so full of errors and misspellings that the publisher would risk running out of ink with which to print "[*sic*]" if all mistakes were so identified; consequently the author has generally included illustrative quotations without correction or comment.

WWW.MEDHELP.ORG, saying, *Sometimes I curl up in a feeble position grabbing my head and holding it with my knees.* This, too, makes perfect nonsense—the headache was so bad that it made her curl up feebly, like a helpless fetus. How can someone who loves language not find that delightful?

We've all made such flubs, at one time or another. The particular pleasure that one gets when one discovers a modern malapropism in the wild comes in part from ferreting out the logic that underlies it. This dictionary's entries attempt to do just that, where it can be deduced, and offer speculation where it can't. Admittedly, sometimes the mistakes are simply *homophones* (like-sounding words), or the originator is the victim of a spell-check program that "corrects" a mere typo (such as *sinch*) into a word that means something else entirely (*synch* instead of the intended *cinch*).

Many malapropisms are figures of speech and can be comically envisioned, which adds to their charm. It is, for example, hard to resist the picture of someone *exercising his demons*. This dictionary helps the process along by illustrating what some of the mistakes suggest.

But the point here isn't to shame the malapropagandists: It's to amuse and inform those of us who care about words. You probably picked it up because you, too, delight in discovering the creative misuse of language; you are interested not only in knowing that *butt naked* is a malapropism but also in how the more standard *buck naked* might have come to be. Perhaps, like me, you are an oft-scorned punster, or you're a crossword-puzzler, or you're the demon proofreader who keeps your office's communications typo-free and knows that *anal retentive* does not take a hyphen unless it is used as a compound adjective.

In any event, this book is for you. So, without further adieu, and with no alterior motive, here are illustrated malapropisms *and nauseam* to peak your interest. I hope you are awaiting them with baited breath.

—Robert Alden Rubin

a note on terminology

This dictionary is one writer's literary reading of lists of common malapropisms and does not aspire to be a formal work of scientific linguistics. However, definitions of some basic terms may help you better understand certain entries. Cross-references to these terms are printed in SMALL CAPS *in the dictionary. Cross-references to other malapropisms are also in* SMALL CAPS.

COGNATES—A word's parallels in other, related languages; the meanings are often not identical.

COLLOQUIAL—Ordinary language, not intended to be literary or formal.

DIALECT—A version of a language, often different and less formal than STANDARD USAGE.

EGGCORN—A MALAPROPISM that nonetheless makes some sense, even if it changes the original words or phrases that inspired it.

ETYMOLOGY—The historical development of words and their meanings, and the study of that development.

FOLK ETYMOLOGY—Popular understanding of a word's origins that may be unrelated to its actual origins. An example would be *acorn*, which was long thought to be a combination of English's *oak* and *corn*. In fact, *acorn* derives from languages that predate English, and it essentially meant *wild seeds from unenclosed lands*.

HOMONYM—A word or phrase that is spelled the same as another but has a different meaning and sometimes a different pronunciation.

HOMOPHONE—A word or phrase that is pronounced the same (or nearly so) as another but may be spelled differently and has a different meaning.

IDIOM—A phrase whose meaning might be hard to deduce from its components but is commonly understood by speakers of a language (e.g., *from here on in*).

MALAPROPISM—A word or phrase that has been mistaken for another, usually because of its sound rather than its meaning (e.g., mistaking *tambourine* for *trampoline*); sometimes called Fay-Cutler Malapropisms.

METAPHOR—A figure of speech that represents one thing (*love*) by another (*a red, red rose*); compare SIMILE.

MONDEGREEN—A misheard line in a song or poem, such as hearing *and Lady Mondegreen* when the actual verse is *and laid him on the green*.

PORTMANTEAU—Two words blended to make a new one (e.g., *motor + hotel = motel*).

PUN—A deliberate play on words as opposed to the unintentional MALAPROPISM.

REANALYSIS—The mental process by which a speaker justifies an EGGCORN to himself or herself (e.g., believing *doesn't know me from atom* refers to elemental particles, not the Bible).

SIMILE—A figure of speech in which one thing is said to be *like* another (*you're like the Mona Lisa*); compare META-PHOR.

SLANG—Informal language used by a particular group, such as teenagers or college students.

SPOONERISM—Transposing parts of words (e.g., *a blushing crow* for *a crushing blow*).

STANDARD USAGE—Linguists tend to avoid saying something is "incorrect," and some argue that a native speaker of a language by definition cannot make "errors" in it; instead they distinguish between *standard* and *nonstandard* conventions of usage.

key to the entries

(1) **coma**, Oxford

(2) v: (3) *serial coma, lapse into a comma.* (4) Rarely an (5) EGG-CORN, often a PUN, and sometimes a spelling error in which the *o-m-m* of *comma* is heard as that in *commingle* rather than as that in *comment*. An *Oxford coma* might occur after a long lecture, but more probably before the last of a series of three or more such lectures. • (6) *In the case of the Oxford coma, suggest that common sense and style govern its usage.*

(7) WWW.RAGAN.COM • (8) 17 MAY 2014

1. **headword:** Listed alphabetically. Phrases containing a malapropism, such as *cutting age*, are alphabetized by the nonstandard word or words (e.g., ***age***, *cutting*). The headword is printed in bold.

2. v: Indicates that variants are included in the entry.

3. *Variants*: Variants of the malapropism, printed in italics.

4. Main entry: Discusses the semantics of the entry, and word and phrase origins.

5. CROSS-REFERENCE: Refers to definitions on pages 7–9 and/or to other entries.

6. *Recent example*: An example of the usage, as found on the Internet.

7. URL: Partial URL of the source of the example.

8. DATE RETRIEVED: Date the example was retrieved (not the date it was written).

a

adieu, without further

V: *much adieu.* Conflation of *adieu* (goodbye) with *ado* (complicated doings, ceremony) to mean "without saying anything more." • *Without further adieu . . . the next remix album is . . . *drumroll* Animal Crossing!*

SHINSHUINBLOOM.TUMBLR.COM • 14 MAR 2014

much adieu

age, cutting

Mixes *cutting edge,* a METAPHOR for technological newness, with *modern age,* a characterization of recent history connoting up-to-date technology and attitudes. • *In businesses I bring cutting age innovation, to assist leadership and their teams transform themselves and their business.*

WWW.EVENTBRITE.COM • 20 MAR 2014

Alcatraz around my neck, like an

A SIMILE that confuses a notorious prison with the neckwear of the speaker in Samuel Taylor Coleridge's famous poem *The*

Alcatraz around your neck

Rime of the Ancient Mariner; the mariner is notorious for killing an *albatross*, and his fellow sailors consequently force him to wear it in penance. • *I always found a job to be like an Alcatraz around my neck.*

WWW.NPAPER-WEHAA.COM • 3 MAY 2014

all be darned

V: *all be damned.* Mixes up expressions of anger (such as *darn it all!*) and surprise (such as *I'll be darned!*) to suggest something so surprising that everybody should be darned, or damned. • *I mentioned a pink-eyed pea (cow pea) that my mentor, John Neal used to make a risotto with. All be darned if they didn't grow them. . . .*

WWW.RUEDUMAINERESTAURANT.COM • 9 APR 2014

alterior motive

Merges *alternative* (other) with *ulterior* (hidden) to mean *other motive.* • *I don't have an alterior motive and I am not paid to do this.*

AMYSHAHMD.COM • 9 APR 2014

optical allusion

allusion, optical

An *allusion* refers to something without naming it directly, whereas an *illusion* is something the senses misperceive. So a drawing that nods to the work of M. C. Escher might be an *optical allusion* to *optical illusions.* Many *allusions* are *illusory,* but this mistake rarely qualifies as an EGGCORN. • *Another optical allusion, if you look careful and long enough, you will see a concealed weapon!*

WWW.FIELDANDSTREAM.COM • 23 JUL 2014

and absurdum, *reductio*

English's *and* often gets mixed up with the Latin *ad* (*to* or *on*), as in the following example, as well as in AND HOMINEM and AND NAUSEAM. This EGGCORN suggests something *small and absurd*. The standard phrase, *reductio ad absurdum*, means something slightly different: simplifying an argument to its essence to demonstrate its absurdity. • *If you have a copy of* Lincoln Murder Conspiracies *see the chapter titled "Reductio and Absurdum."*

WWW.LINCOLN-ASSASSINATION.COM • 23 JUL 2014

and a while, once

Confuses *once in a while* with phrases such as *once and for all*, *and a while (longer)*, *awhile*, *once and future*, *once and again*, etc. "Once in a" is usually pronounced "Once 'n uh," as if it were "and a," adding to the confusion. • *FX is also concerned about why it is important to make room in your life for alcohol every once and a while.*

WWW.TEENHEALTHFX.COM • 10 JUL 2014

and cheek, tongue

Possibly confuses *tongue in cheek* (being ironic or flippant) with *tongue-and-groove* (a type of joint often used for flooring and siding). Flippant people are considered "cheeky," and their speech might be a case of "tongue" and "cheek." • *[W]ith all due respect, unless that was a tongue and cheek remark, I'm afraid you been downing more wine than I previously had thought.*

WWW.BERWYNTALK.COM • 4 AUG 2014

and chief, commander

Commander and chief is a description, not a military rank. Britain's Prince Charles, for example, was given the rank of commander (and later admiral) in the Royal Navy, and may one day be king, the largely ceremonial *chief* executive of the state, but would not exercise authority as *commander in chief* of the UK armed forces, a rank with which the description is often confused. • *Why would a man who was running for the office of Commander and Chief of the US Armed Forces refuse to discuss his service in the military?*

WWW.HEREINREALITY.COM • 17 MAY 2014

and hell, sure

Sure and hell confuses *sure as hell* with expostulations such as *hell, yes!* Some eighteenth-century sermons refer to hell as being "sure," influenced by Calvinistic beliefs that people were naturally depraved and doomed to hell unless saved by divine grace. • *My car has NO creature comforts, but it sure and hell is a blast to drive. . . .*

WWW.YELLOWBULLET.COM • 1 AUG 2014

and hominem

V: *and homonym.* The *argumentum ad hominem* (Latin for *argument "to the man"*) criticizes an opponent's character rather than ideas, the way some politicians discredit their rivals; *and hominem* implies that the attacks are something of an afterthought. • The Crimson's Confidential Guide to Harvard *would be a more valuable publication if there were less unsubstantiated editorializing and fewer and hominem attacks on particular Instructors.*

WWW.THECRIMSON.COM • 10 APR 2014

and nauseam

V: *and infinitum, and hoc.* The Latin *ad nauseam* translates as "something repeated so often it becomes sickening." Many EGGCORN-ists are thinking not of the translation (literally *to the point of nausea*) but rather of the simple idea that it's something extra, or *et cetera,* the Latin phrase with which it's often confused. • *But with nature versus nurture, the dichotomy is all in the eye of the beholder, and the real situation is much more complex (as is pointed out* and nauseam*).*

BOOKS.GOOGLE.COM • 10 APR 2014

and point, case

In point was a seventeenth-century expression meaning *pertinent,* so *case in point* meant a *pertinent case.* It's now confused with two associated items—a *case* and a *point,* much as *set and match* are associated with tennis victory. • *One case and point, Rodney King. May he rest in peace.*

THEGRIO.COM • 13 MAY 2014

and tolerant, lactose

V: *lack toast and tolerant, lack toast intolerant.* You might hear *lactose* as an adjective like *verbose,* but one that has something to do with digestion rather than with wordiness. True *lactose intolerance* describes difficulty digesting milk products. The Internet's *Eggcorn Database* identifies the variant *lack toast and tolerant* as a "rare double

EGGCORN"—but most of the examples that Google turns up are intended to be funny and aren't true MALAPROP- ISMS. • *That summer I became lactose and tolerant which helps.*

WWW.PETA.ORG • 25 SEPT 2014

annunciate

Annunciate is an antique word meaning *to announce* (now used mostly to describe Gabriel's announcement of the miracle of the Virgin Mary's pregnancy) that gets con- fused with *enunciate* (*to pronounce* a word). • *The quick fix is to take a few moments off mic, alone in the hall before your performance and read the piece slowly, forcing yourself to annunciate each word fully.*

WWW.SOUNDSWRITE.CA • 4 MAY 2014

another words

V: *in another words.* Mistaken for *in other words,* which is used as a restatement. The MALAPROPISM has the logic typi- cal of an EGGCORN, conveying the sense of *another word is . . . ,* or *in another [person's] words.* • *Can dogs remember things? (in another words are they smart?)*

ANSWERS.YAHOO.COM • 11 APR 2014

ansister

Since both *sister* and *ancestor* are family-related, this mistake seems natural—or "unnatural," as the case may be: The only way one's sister could be one's ancestor is through incest. • *I'm looking to see if callie or calli a[—] is my ansister.*

WWW.GENEALOGYSEARCH.COM • 8 APR 2014

a posable thumb

V: *a poseable thumb.* A professional hand model would have *a posable thumb*; only primates have *opposable thumbs* with which they can touch the fingers on their hands. • *Ok, barring our posable thumb and their lengthy tails, I've heard it said that canine anatomy is very similar to human anatomy.*

BOARDS.STRAIGHTDOPE.COM • 21 JUL 2014

approach, above

V: *beyond approach.* The STANDARD USAGES, *above reproach* and *beyond reproach* (criticism), perhaps imply a disrespectful *approach* (drawing near to someone) because *reproach* sounds similar and has a similar ETYMOLOGY. • *Paul urges Timothy to insist that an elder is above approach.*

WWW.TEKNIA.COM • 14 MAR 2014.

assault, take it with a grain

A grain of salt proverbially makes unpalatable food more savory, and when used figuratively, it makes hard-to-swallow (or unbelievable) news a little easier to digest. The EGGCORN *a grain assault* accomplishes this with a lot of roughage instead. • *Advice? Take it with a grain assault, but don't balk at the advice from people who have some idea of what they're talking about.*

a grain assault

WWW.ZYNGAPLAYERFORUMS.COM • 11 APR 2014

assume, I would just

To *assume* means to infer or suppose something but not state it. *I'd just as soon* means *I'd rather* or *I'd prefer*. It becomes an EGGCORN for those who would rather keep their preferences unstated. • *Sure, I'd gladly accept a dozen red*

*roses from my main squeeze on February fourteenth but I'd
just assume he surprises me with a few giant sunflowers on
any random day of the week.*

DASHOFLES.COM • 11 APR 2014

don't know him from atom

atom, doesn't know (you) from

Confuses *Adam*, the generic man, and *atom*, the generic elemental particle. • *I have never seen a [pain management] Doctor giving high dosages of any medication right of the bat, they don't know you from atom, and they like to protect themselves against drug seekers. . . .*

WWW.DAILYSTRENGTH.ORG • 9 APR 2014

auger well for

V: *all goes well for.* An *auger* (a tool with a pointy end) and the verb *augur* (from an *augury*, which means an omen, and can have a point to make about the end) are confused here. • *McGraw-Hill Breakup Augers Well for CFO Callahan.*

BLOGS.WSJ.COM/CFO/2012 • 12 APR 2014

away, anchors

Confuses a ship getting *under way* with casting off moorings (which, unlike anchors, are left behind), and with the phrase *anchors a-weigh.* To *weigh anchor* means to free an anchor from the bottom and bring it aboard. • *At a young age she sang along with the Lawrence Welk show, and at age 11, learned to play piano and sing "Anchors Away" in tribute to her older brother, then a Naval Academy midshipman.*

EN.WIKIPEDIA.ORG • RETRIEVED 8 APR 2014

a way, right

Confuses getting somewhere as directly as possible, *right away*, with the legal right to pass across someone else's land, a *right-of-way*. • *Right past his house he has a gate crossing the right a way and he allows his cows to roam across the right away.*

WWW.EXPERTLAW.COM • 24 JUL 2014

awkword

What language flub could be more *awkward*? This entire dictionary owes its existence to awkwords. • *Well, I think the best way to deal with those awkword silence moments you are bound to have in a conversation is to be honest about it and not try to use some preprogrammed default escape routes.*

WWW.ROOSHV.COM • 11 APR 2014

axle, double (triple, etc.)

Wheels rotate on an *axle*, much as skaters rotate when performing the spinning jump named after Norwegian *Axel* Paulsen. Only the latter is judged at the Olympics, however. • *The system is used to help figure skaters build confidence as they start to learn new figure skating maneu-*

double axle

vers, jumps, tricks and lifts . . . [including] Single Axle, Double Axle, Triple Axle, Inside Axles, One Foot Axles, etc.

WWW.JUMPHARNESS.COM • 11 APR 2014

backpeddle

Brakeless early bicycles and unicycles required *backpedaling* (resisting the forward motion of the pedals) to stop or reverse. The action of athletes running backward, which resembles that of backpedaling unicyclists, took on that name. *Peddling* means selling, so *backpeddling* is usually just a spelling error unless it conveys the idea of going back on a sale or deal. • *Saffer appeared to backpeddle on the agreement to give the humane society more than $20,000 left in the animal control budget.*

PCH.STPARCHIVE.COM • 12 APR 2014

bailing wire

Baling wire binds *bales*. The wire isn't used for *bailing* water, but the *OED* suggests that the METAPHOR of bales being dropped through a barn loft's trapdoor came to be used for jumping from an airplane. *Baling out* therefore morphed into *bailing out* (as water is tossed from a boat), which is now STANDARD USAGE. So there is a connection. • *Number 8 on the greatest tools of all times list that most versatile of all binders, Bailing Wire.*

WWW.LIFEHACK.ORG • 12 APR 2014

baited breath

Bated or *abated breath* (holding one's breath or breathing shallowly) was a term used by Shakespeare for "nervous anticipation." *Baited breath* suggests a fisherman who waits anxiously for a strike, or maybe an enticingly scented mouthwash. It's doubtful that Beyoncé would be attracted by the scent of fishing worms, if the following example is accurate. • *Millions of Beyoncé fans are waiting with baited breath.*

baited breath

PAGESIX.COM • 12 APR 2014

ball (your) eyes out

British English associates *bawling* with loud animal sounds, whereas American English associates it with loud weeping, particularly by children. The EGGCORN suggests an image of crying so hard that one's eyeballs pop out, a condition known as *proptosis*. The expression may also be confused with one used to describe aggressive sex: *balling her eyes out.* • *Check the trailer below and ball your eyes out.*

STICKSXSTONES.COM • 12 APR 2014

ban together

Many people leave out the *d* when pronouncing and spelling *band together*. However, *ban together*, if being used to describe a protest action, does make a sort of sense. • *'Discrimination is a threat we can all stop if we ban together to make an impact that can change our world for the better and create a better future for the children of America and the people of today,' Shay said.*

WWW.9NEWS.COM • 12 APR 2014

To who,
or
not to who...

bard owl

bard owl

Bards and the *barred owl* (*Strix varia*) are both known for their songs. The poet and playwright Shakespeare is often known as the Bard, for his lovely verses. The owl's call is typically rendered in English as "Who cooks for you? Who cooks for you all?" • *The environmental studies and creative writing major first heard her own call to nature after a year-long encounter with a bard owl that sat on a branch in her backyard.*

DAILYEMERALD.COM • 11 APR 2014

bare the brunt

V: *bear the blunt, bare the blunt. Bear the brunt* means to absorb the force of an attack or blow. The MALAPROPISM suggests a *bare*, unprotected self's or group's enduring it. *Bear* and *bare* get mixed up a lot, since one means something fierce and wild, and one describes something primitive and naked. • *The firm has been looking at axing around 1,000 jobs across its shipyards, in Scotland, Plymouth and Portsmouth, but now it looks like the Hampshire yard will bare the brunt of the cuts.*

WWW.DAILYECHO.CO.UK • 13 APR 2014

bare witness

Four hundred years ago the King James Bible proclaimed, "Ye sent unto John, and he bare witness unto the truth"

(John 5:33). For King James the past tense of *bear* was *bare*, not the modern *bore*. These days, testifying can make you feel exposed, so *bare witness* makes some sense, and the phrase might also convey the simple (*bare*) act of witnessing. •

bare witness

The Christian community should be capable of full agreement within, able to bare witness to Christ to the outside world, to prevent any of its members from suffering and misery.

WWW.CATHOLICANADA.COM • 29 APR 2014

barreled, no holds

V: *no holds barrel, no holes barred.* Barrels typically lack handles, so all are *no holds barrels.* Wrestling *bars* (forbids) certain dangerous *holds,* except in no-rules matches. The phrase may be confused with *to barrel* (to move unstoppably, as casks do when rolling downhill) or *double-barreled* (a double shotgun blast). • *If it was a full-force, no holds barreled attack from start to end, it would clearly just get boring after a few tracks.*

WWW.METALRAGE.COM • 29 APR 2014

base voice

V: *base guitar, base fiddle,* etc. *Base* and *bass* share an ETYMOLOGY, but *base* refers to lowness of height or stature, and *bass* to lowness of tone. *Bass,* from the Italian *basso,* was formerly pronounced to rhyme with "glass." *Base* can also refer to lowness of character; since most opera villains sing the low part, the bad guy is usually a base bass. • *A deep, relaxing, base voice in a blue shirt instructs you on how to give a proper back massage. Enjoy!*

WWW.SOOTHETUBE.COM • 2 MAY 2014

batter an eyelid

The standard *didn't bat an eye* (or *bat an eyelid* or *eyelash*) means showing no surprise, not refraining from *battering* someone's eye black and blue, or breading it for deep frying. • *Our tutor . . . was extremely friendly, helpful and most importantly patience. He didn't even batter an eyelid when the clubs were referred to as "sticks."*

WWW.LUXURYTRAVELBIBLE.COM • 2 MAY 2014

batter down the hatches

Battering hatches might suggest hammering them shut rather than using canvas secured by wooden *battens*. • *The winds that hammer at our buildings mean we sometimes have to batter down the hatches. . . .*

VISIT.SHETLAND.ORG • 3 DEC 2014

bear (her) fangs

Bearing (carrying) one's fangs is perhaps less threatening than *baring* (showing) them, but in both cases they're handy and ready for use. • *Instead of a reckoning, we're treated to a wine-drunk Cersei in full-on fang-bearing mode (as is her wont) mocking Jaime's apparent loyalty to the Stark clan and questioning why Catelyn decided to let him go, before demanding Sansa's head.*

WWW.THEDAILYBEAST.COM • 28 APR 2014

bear-knuckle fight

V: *bear-handed fight.* Bears fight with their claws and teeth, not their *bare knuckles*, which makes them particularly dangerous when there are *no holds* BARRELED • *The most contrived sequence comes during one of the bear knuckle fight sequences as a battered Ali looks down for the count until Stephanie shows up and inspires him to victory. . . .*

bear knuckle fight

YORKSHIRETIMES.CO.UK • 2 MAY 2014

beat and path, off the

A *beat*, the sort that a cop patrols, is a regular routine, so *beat and path* makes some sense and may actually improve on the clichéd phrase *off the beaten path*. Also confused with *offbeat*, a musical term. • *We are life long travellers and both prefer the off the beat and path locations where you can settle in and relax and that is what we tried to create here for you.*

WWW.QIPALAWAN.COM • 5 JUN 2014

beat on, draw a

V: *get a beat on.* A *bead* is the sight affixed to the barrel of many guns; the shooter lines it up with the sight closer to the trigger and *draws a bead on* a target. The EGGCORN may confuse it with rhythm, or a reporter's or a cop's *beat* targeting a certain area, or a beating that someone undergoes. • *That allowed West Virginia's defense to draw a beat on young Tiger quarterback Tajh Boyd.*

WWW.WVUSPORTS.COM • 3 DEC 2014

beckon call

V: *back and call, beacon call, beckoned call.* Early modern English used *beck* as both a noun and a verb to indicate both a come-hither gesture and the act of doing so. The modern MALAPROPISM *beckon call* should be *beckoning and call.* A *beacon* figuratively calls one home. • *Mrs. Shores was unable to care for herself. Her son was at her beckon call, 24 hours a day, seven days a week.*

ROANOKE-CHOWANNEWSHERALD.COM • 18 MAY 2014

beckon the question

Begging the question is a logical fallacy by which one simply asserts a proposition is true without adequately explaining why (for example, "Everyone wants the Cabbage Patch Kids because they're the hottest toy of the season"). It is often misused by speakers who think it means *asking the question.* Parliamentarians ask for a vote by *calling the question.* This EGGCORN triply mixes up those senses with that of BECKON CALL. • *There are just some tasty morsels that beckon the question, "Are you going to eat that?"*

WWW.ALAMODEUS.NET • 3 MAY 2014

beknighted

To be *benighted* is to be in the dark, so this might be a mere HOMOPHONE error, unless you're describing someone whose ignorance is like that of a knight in the "dark" ages of medieval times. • *You'll perhaps forgive me if I don't take beknighted little orange farmer, Ricke Kress, at face value when he suggests he's fighting against the big, bad FDA, consumer groups, and environmentalists.*

DILETTANTECOCKTAILER.BLOGSPOT.COM • 3 MAY 2014

bellweather

A *wether* was a castrated ram (the word comes from the same root as *veal*), and shepherds often put a bell on the wether that led the flock home. *Bellwether* now connotes a leading indicator, and most people think it has to do with *weather* forecasting. • *It is time to recognize the serious California drought for what it is: a bellweather of things to come.*

SCIENCEBLOGS.COM • 3 MAY 2014

bemused

Confuses *musing* and *amused*, intending to convey the sense of *detached, thoughtful amusement* rather than the dictionary definition, which is *dazed* or *perplexed*. The EGG-CORN's meaning actually seems to be winning its battle with STANDARD USAGE; some dictionary definitions include it. • *[Einstein's] scientific breakthroughs were so breathtaking that his gentle, bemused expression and riot of white hair have come to symbolize genius in the popular imagination.*

WWW.AMNH.ORG •

3 MAY 2014

besiege you

Confuses *besiege* (a military action) with *beseech* (an act of pleading). An influential person

besiege you

might be *besieged* by *beseechers*. • *My fellow Americans, I besiege you to take a closer look at this situation of immigration.*

MYDD.COM • 3 MAY 2014

be who of (you)

Behoove (spelled *behove* in Britain) means *to be incumbent upon one to do one's duty*. The MALAPROPISM turns it into an expression of self-definition—an action that defines *who* you are and what you are consequently expected to do. • *An opportunity may be appealing but if it takes you off course from what God has called you to then it would be who of you to take some time and ensure that the opportunity is in line with the direction God wants you to go.*

DANIELDBLOG.WORDPRESS.COM • 3 MAY 2014

black and red fish

Blackened redfish, a Cajun dish popularized by celebrity chef Paul Prudhomme, calls for fillets of *redfish* (red snapper), seasoned with *black and red* pepper and other herbs and spices, seared in a cast-iron skillet. • *Roux Bistro boasts its black-and-red fish po' boy and private tastings for special clients.*

WWW.TRAVELAGENTCENTRAL.COM •

6 MAY 2014

blackmale

Blackmail has no historical connection to *black males* (who get blamed for everything, it seems), nor to the postal service. The

blackmale

OED says *male* or *maile* was medieval Scots DIALECT for *rent*, and *the blackmaile* referred to raids by highland Scottish warlords who demanded what we'd call "protection money" (or blackmail) from the lowland farmers whose homes they threatened. Medieval English nobles, on the other hand, sometimes demanded payment from their vassals in silver, which was known as *white rent*. • *He is bullying me and has blackmaled me but noone will do anything about it.*

PRODUCTFORUMS.GOOGLE.COM • 6 MAY 2014

bloodgeon

Linguists don't know how *bludgeon* originated. It resembles the English nouns *truncheon* and *cudgel*, and it possibly comes from a Cornish word for a piece of wood, or a French word for a club, or even (as the EGGCORN does) the *blood* that a truncheon's *bludgeon*ing blow often produces. • *I'm surprised that the original poster has not yet been bloodgeoned to death by some of the people around this forum.*

WWW.ELECTRICALAUDIO.COM • 8 MAY 2014

bobwire

v: *barred wire, bared wire.* The *OED* cites novelist John Steinbeck's use of *bobwire* in *The Grapes of Wrath* to illustrate rural-Oklahoma DIALECT; it's an EGGCORN if you think the barbs of the knotted wires are formed by being *bobbed*. *Barred wire* may mean metal bars or posts used to string the *bared* wire of *barbwire* fences. • *Found a newborn last year that had been dragged over the bobwire fence.*

WWW.CATTLETODAY.COM • 25 SEPT 2014

boggled down

V: *balked down.* Back when most roads weren't paved, cars and wagons often got *bogged down* in mire. The EGG-CORN confuses it with having your mind *boggled* (astonished). • *Can I just say that my mind is boggled down with trying to learn CSS code right now?*

WWW.STUDIOCALICO.COM • 9 MAY 2014

bold-faced lie

V: *bear-faced lie.* Perhaps a lie printed in *boldface* type, or told boldly. The expression *barefaced lie* (an undisguised lie) goes back to eighteenth-century England, from which it spread to the American frontier and got mixed up with *baldface* whiskey (bad whiskey that stung like a bald-faced hornet) and became a *bald-faced lie.* • *In his complaint, Parisot called Gaetz's comment a "bold-faced lie" and said he'd never filled out a comment form to speak at the meeting.*

WWW.NWFDAILYNEWS.COM • 9 MAY 2014

Bombay chest

A rounded chest that gets its name from its bomblike shape (*bombé* in France, where the design originated) rather than from the Indian city of *Bombay* (now Mumbai). The exotic city has some marketing appeal, however: *Bombé chests* are sold as *Bombay chests* by retailers such as Walmart. • *International Caravan Windsor 5–Drawer Hand Carved Bombay Chest . . . $208.34.*

WWW.WALMART.COM • 9 MAY 2014

bonified

No bones about it: *bona fide* comes from the Latin *bona fides* (good faith), which assures one that something is the real thing. Perhaps *bonified* takes the same Latin word for *good*, or its French COGNATE (*bon*), and adds *-ified*, much as *ver* (from the Latin *verus*, truth) becomes *verified*, so that the EGGCORN basically means *good-ified*. • *So the new Miss Jamaica Universe is a bonified Rastafarian!*

JDIDTHOUGHTS.BLOGSPOT.COM • 8 MAY 2014

boots trap

A computer *boots up*, shorthand for the computer process originally known as *bootstrapping*—jumping into action from a dead start, as in *pulling yourself up by your bootstraps*. Some technical writers hear it as a *trapping* procedure that follows the *booting* procedure. • *implemented a modal of twitter boots trap . . . it works fine when i dont put it in my site.*

STACKOVERFLOW.COM • 25 SEPT 2014

bough, shot over the

A warship fires a warning *shot over the bow* of a less powerful ship to demand compliance. The EGGCORN *a shot over the bough* would perhaps be the land-based equivalent, in which one combatant fires a warning shot over another's trees. • *Reading this now, 20 years on, one might suspect Lane's missive as a shot over the bough of a certain type of poetry book common in the Canadian canon. . . .*

PURITAN-MAGAZINE.COM • 10 MAY 2014

bowl in a china shop

A *bowl* is more likely than a *bull* to be found *in a china shop*. It's difficult to determine where the proverbial bull originated, but TV's *MythBusters* show recently put the saying to the test, and found that bulls are surprisingly nimble;

bowl in a china shop

dishes and bowls were left intact when a bull *walked the* ISLES • *Well there was no unity at all because Mc-Chrystal was a bowl in a china shop.*

WWW.VETERANSTODAY.COM • 10 MAY 2014

brand, raisin

The *bran* (husk) of a grain's kernel got its name from Old French, whereas *brand* (a burned mark, a burning branch) was a German word. *Raisin Bran* is part of several common brand names, so confusion is common, too. • *Calories in Raisin Brand based on the calories, fat, protein, carbs and other nutrition information submitted for Raisin Brand.*

WWW.SPARKPEOPLE.COM • 4 JUN 2014

branded about

V: *brandied about.* Confuses *bandy* (to casually pass on an idea or rumor) and *bruit* (to spread a rumor widely), both often used with *about.* The variant adds a dash of high-proof alcohol to the casual talk. • *John Cena's (one of Vince McMahon's kids) name has been branded about for the lead—but it's early days.*

WWW.MOVIESONLINE.CA • 10 MAY 2014

bread and breakfast

Something of a SPOONERISM. Few *bed and breakfast* inns ask you to sleep on a loaf, however pillowy. A 2004

Finnish art festival did hire nine unemployed men to sleep on a *bed* made of sliced *bread* as a statement about the politics of food. • *Inn Boonsboro's fan page began with a link to the April 30, 2010 New York Times article, "Maryland's Civil War Country Seeks a Softer Side," which featured the restored 18th century bread-and-breakfast inn.*

WWW.EXAMINER.COM • 10 MAY 2014

breath, length and

Often a mere spelling error, unless it conveys not a measurement of broadness but the sense of airiness and "room to breathe." • *Mayo has so much to offer for photographers and on this workshop we'll explore the length and breath of this wild and beautiful county on Ireland's West Coast.*

WWW.APERTUREWEST.COM • 10 MAY 2014

brunt-force trauma

V: *brunt-force drama*, *blunt-force drama*. Confuses a medical term, *blunt-force trauma* (the damage to a body from an impact that does not penetrate the skin), with a description of what accompanies the *brunt* (main impact) of a blow. • *In hockey, most head injuries are caused by brunt force trauma to the head region such as during a body check, a high stick to the head or when you have a hard fall on the ice.*

WWW.EXPLORECURIOCITY.ORG • 11 MAY 2014

bruted about

A HOMOPHONE. Something *bruited about* is a rumor widely spread, which can be *brutal* indeed if the rumor is untrue. • *In one of the other discussions it was bruted about that if Smith had moved further south he might have avoided ice.*

WWW.ENCYCLOPEDIA-TITANICA.ORG • 27 JUN 2014

bud of the joke

Subject of most Cheech and Chong movies. The EGGCORN confuses *bud* (a flowery or leafy outgrowth) with *butt* (which originally meant a target). Both words have meanings that suggest something low from which humor blossoms. • *"We get quite a special show, seeing his family members who are the bud of the joke are often in the audience."*

WWW.BURNIE.NET • 11 MAY 2014

bullion cube

v: *gold bouillon. Bouillon* cubes get their name from the French word for *boiling,* and so does gold *bullion* (gold is heated to a molten state before being poured into ingots). Both are cuboid in shape, but one makes better soup. • *Discover all the tastiest beef bullion cube recipes, hand-picked by home chefs and other food lovers like you.*

WWW.PINTEREST.COM • 11 MAY 2014

busting tables

busting tables

Someone who *bused tables* was originally called an *omnibus*, because he carried everything; hence the verb *to bus*. But *busting tables* after a meal makes a certain sense, too, as the opposite of *setting tables* before it. • *Before graduating, Paula dropped out to*

pursue her show business career. Some of her early jobs in-
clude busting tables and working as a bicycle messenger.

WWW.CELEBRITYNETWORTH.COM • 11 MAY 2014

butt, nip it in the

Geese sometimes em-
ploy this strategy with
strangers who invade
their turf. *Nip in the
bud* is an IDIOM bor-
rowed from horticulturists. They postpone a plant's

nip it in the butt

unproductive blooming by cutting off (*nipping*) buds,
diverting its energy to growth rather than to flowering.
Both have the effect of stopping something unwanted. •
*Better nip it in the butt now, or you will really have trouble
later.*

ANSWERS.YAHOO.COM • 8 JUL 2014

buttkiss, (doesn't) know

V: *don't know butkis, doesn't know Butkus.* Many readers today
don't know much about NFL Hall of Fame linebacker
Dick Butkus, who played in the 1960s and '70s. But they
don't know about the Yiddish word *bupkis* (*nothing*) either
and instead equate the expression with the epithet *kiss
my ass* (or *butt*). • *He may (or not) know politics but he know
buttkiss about economics.*

BLOGS.NEWS.COM.AU • 12 MAY 2014

butt naked

V: *but naked.* Linguists debate whether it's *buck naked* or
butt naked. Although *buck naked* is recorded earlier, *butt*

naked is now much more common, and makes more sense. It may be an example of the SMALLCAPS EGGCORN replacing the STANDARD USAGE. The *American Heritage Dictionary* speculates that *buck* may have been a euphemism for the vulgar *butt*. But *buck naked* could well be an old DIALECT expression of unlettered Scots-Irish immigrants to the American South who combined the antique Scottish *buck*, or *bouk* (body, human trunk), and *nakit* (naked), which would make *butt naked* the EGGCORN. • *"I'm butt naked. I've never been so naked before in all my life," Nugent said in pointing out he was not carrying a concealed weapon.*

POLITICALTICKER.BLOGS.CNN.COM • 12 MAY 2014

buy (one's) time

Confuses the expressions *bide one's time* (to wait) and *buy time* (to stall). • *Frankly I don't care anymore and am not really out here selling, just buying my time until the other companies start hiring.*

WWW.CAFEPHARMA.COM • 12 MAY 2014

bye and bye

V: *bye the bye*. Mixes up the old gospel-music term "the sweet *by-and-by*" (someday, heaven, eternity, etc.) with *bye-bye* ("goodbye"), since going to heaven can entail saying "bye-bye" to the people one has known. • *We will understand it better bye and bye.*

WWW.CLEARLIGHT.COM • 12 MAY 2014

byte, sound

Sound bite, which TV producers had coined by the early 1970s to describe short audio snippets for broadcast news stories, referred at the time to analog recordings. The term *byte* has been around since the 1950s to describe digital data. Now that almost all audio is digital, however, *sound bites* are literally composed of *bytes* of data, so there's some sense to the EGGCORN. • *At best they saw a verse printed in the newspaper or heard a sound byte via television and radio news clips.*

WWW.NEWSDAY.CO.TT • 30 JUL 2014

C

cacoughany
Perhaps this confuses a chorus of audience *coughs* before a stage performance with a *cacophony* (a discordant mixture of sounds). • *A cacoughany of swears and shouts topped off with a bag of doritos and a bottle of moutain dew, all wich lasts far into the night.*

WWW.ESCAPISTMAGAZINE.COM • 12 MAY 2014

Cadillac converter
Confuses GM's luxury brand with the *catalytic converter* device required on all US cars to reduce exhaust pollution. *Cadillac* gets its name from the French founder of Detroit, Antoine Laumet de La Mothe

Cadillac converter

Cadillac, who named himself after a French river port. The device uses a chemical *catalyst* to change toxic exhaust particles to less harmful forms. Unfortunately, it will not change your Chevy into a Caddy. • *I'm having a hard time to deciding if I should get the cadillac converter from honda dealership that's going to cost me $1,000 or one from auto zone that's $303.99?*

COMMUNITY.CARTALK.COM • 13 MAY 2014

calvary charge

A spelling error that mixes up the middle letters of *cavalry* (mounted troops). An EGGCORN only in the case of a battle charge likened to the assaults of medieval Crusaders seeking to conquer the holy hill of *Calvary* (Latin for *skull*) in Jerusalem. • *Am I right in thinking that the very last Calvary charge in modern warfare is the Polish horse charge against the invading German army?*

WWW.WW2AIRCRAFT.NET • 13 MAY 2014

cat before the horse

Cart is pronounced like *cat* in such places as Boston. However, *cat before the horse* appears instead of *cart before the horse* often enough to suggest that many writers get the IDIOM wrong, as if one normally prioritized horses over cats. • *I believe fans will have to be a bit patient with Arsene wenger. we cannot put the cat before the horse.*

ARSENALTRANSFERS.CO.UK • 13 MAY 2014

catchitore, chicken

The Italian *cacciatore* means *hunter*, and it comes from the same root as English's *catch*. The *hunter's chicken* recipe is widely known, the Italian word's spelling less so, and the word's beginning with the sound of *catch* may suggest hunting to some cooks. • *chicken catchitore topped with provolone cheese served with cauliflower not the prettiest but mama cooked tonight since i had work sooo late.*

ASHLEYBAR.TUMBLR.COM • 12 MAY 2014

catch nap

Combines *catnap* with the expression *catch forty winks*. • *When you see him on the couch trying to catch a catch nap at 12 noon. . . . go pick him up . . . pet him a bit and set him on the floor.*

ANSWERS.YAHOO.COM • 13 MAY 2014

Catillac

Usually a misspelling or a PUN, but a few examples show up in the wild that assign feline characteristics to the slinky car brand. • *Shop outside the big box, with unique items for catillac mountain from thousands of independent designers and vintage collectors on Etsy.*

WWW.ETSY.COM • 13 MAY 2014

caused (you your) job

Employees can be fired (or terminated) *with cause*, meaning *because they did something bad*. That may help explain this confusion with the expression *cost (you your) job*, which can result if you give your employer *cause*. • *Biggest mistake in Andy Reid's tenure that caused him his job?*

FORUMS.PROSPORTSDAILY.COM • 13 MAY 2014

cease the day

V: *cease the opportunity*. Perhaps confuses two maxims: *carpe diem* (*seize the day*) and *stop and smell the roses*. To *cease the day*, however, would literally be to "stop the day." •

The course was never given a formal name but we find out the main objective is to cease the day.

WWW.STARPULSE.COM • 13 MAY 2014

censor, (smoke, motion, etc.)

V: *censer. Censor* comes from a Latin word, *censēre*, meaning *to judge*, while the correct usage, *sensor*, comes from *sentīre*, *to feel*. A sensor's data can regulate the thing it senses, much as censors regulate speech they hear or read, which may explain the confusion. The variant, *censer*, confuses a device that senses smoke with an incense-burning device that produces it. • *I was able to see that there was water coming from the exhaust so I think that the problem was due to a faulty censor.*

WWW.YBW.COM • 14 MAY 2014

centripedal force

V: *centrifical force.* Sir Isaac Newton coined the words *centripetal* (from the Latin for *fall to the center*) and *centrifugal* (from the Latin for *flee from the center*). How *pedals* figure in *centripetal force* is difficult to pinpoint. Maybe it involves the experience of stepping on the brake pedal as a car goes around a curve and then feeling centripetal force keeping it from spinning out. • *In the fluid dynamics sense, centripedal force refers to the suction process that causes fluids to move inwards and towards the centre in a spiraling whirling path.*

THEIMPLODER.COM • 14 MAY 2014

chalk-full

V: *chock it up to.* Confuses *chockfull* with *chalk it up to. Chockfull* is an old phrase, perhaps coming from *choke-full* or *full to choking. Chalk it up to* comes from chalk tally marks on a slate. *Chock marks* indicate where to put wooden chocks (or wedges) and may be confused with *chalk marks.* • *London School of Economics Study of Piracy Chalk full of Methodology Flaws, Bad Science, and Thoroughly Debunked Theories.*

COPYRIGHTALLIANCE.ORG • 15 MAY 2014

cheese, cut to the

Confuses an expression from TV and movie editing, *cut to the chase* (get to the interesting part), with *cut the cheese*, a joking euphemism for farting that refers to aromatic cheese. The writer may also have in mind something akin to "get to the substance of the argument." • *My job is mostly programming / fixing bugs / developing features . . . software engineering to cut to the cheese.*

cut to the cheese

WORKPLACE.STACKEXCHANGE.COM • 15 MAY 2014

chiffonrobe

Confuses a *chiffon robe*, a garment made of sheer chiffon fabric, with a *chifforobe*, a piece of furniture in which to hang it. *Chifforobe* is a PORTMANTEAU word that combines the drawers of a *chiffonier* and the hanging space of a *wardrobe.* • *Antique wooden chiffonrobe with two ornamental doors—drawers on one side, rack for hangers on the other.*

BALTIMORE.CRAIGSLIST.ORG • 8 JUN 2014

cholester oil

Cholesterol is more like alcohol than like oil. Greek *kholē* means *bile*, and *-sterol* means that it is a compound related to *steroids*. But high levels in the body may indeed come from overconsuming certain oils and fats. • *I'm not sure what that means in the long run but they may have to change my Zocor cholester-oil lowering drug.*

DAVEMAN.BLOGDRIVE.COM • 15 MAY 2014

chomp at the bit

The antique English word for biting down, *champ*, is giving way to the COLLOQUIAL *chomp*, much as *stamping* is giving way to *stomping*—at least where feet are concerned. *Champ* survives in describing chewing by livestock, and especially in the equestrian expression *champing at the bit*, where it's still a METAPHOR for impatience. *Chomping* suggests actual biting. • *Why does my horse chomp at the bit so much?*

FORUM.CYBERHORSE.COM.AU • 15 MAY 2014

click

The French *clique* meant a clicking or clapping sound. Its use in English to describe exclusive groups comes from French *claques*, groups paid to applaud at theatres. Americans, pronouncing it "click" instead of the French "cleek," are thus returning the word to its roots. • *First off I would like to say high school clicks are way over rated. People think they are cool because they're in with the cool kids so to speak.*

THECRAZYTHINGSABOUTLIFE.BLOGSPOT.COM • 15 MAY 2014

climatic battle

Debate over global warming is a *climatic battle*. It will reach a *climax*, becoming a *climactic battle*, when New York and other coastal cities start drowning. The EGGCORN conveys the sense that things are going to get hot. • Hellboy *creator Mike Mignola of Manhattan Beach appears amidst climatic battle!*

WWW.EASYREADERNEWS.COM • 15 MAY 2014

clusterphobia

The condition takes its name from the Latin *claustrum*—a lock or bolt—and describes someone nervous about being locked in a small space. But a *cluster* of

clusterphobia

people can indeed produce both *claustrophobia* and *agoraphobia* (fear of crowds). • *We've only been here a couple of hours, and the combination of cluster-phobia and hypothermia is already setting in.*

WWW.NOWTORONTO.COM • 23 JUL 2014

coal-hearted

For *cold-hearted*. Merle Travis sang of the love of mining that would "seep in your soul/ Till the stream of your blood runs black as the coal," which certainly sounds *coal-hearted*. Usually a PUN, not an EGGCORN. • *I even played a game that nearly made me, a coal-hearted and media-saturated writer, cry.*

WWW.BUZZFEED.COM • 15 MAY 2014

cognitive dissidence

Dissidence means *dissent*. The MALAPROPISM confuses it with the theory of *cognitive dissonance*, which describes the mental turmoil that comes from believing two contradictory things at once. Some psychologists don't buy into the theory, which would make their skepticism *cognitive dissidence*. • *It was like my system was shocked last night. I guess this is what "cognitive dissidence" really feels like.*

WWW.FAIRMORMONSUPPORT.ORG • 15 MAY 2014

cohorts with, in

Mixes up three phrases with similar meanings: *Cohort* meant a Roman military unit and today means a group or a person's supporters. *In cahoots with* may derive from a French word for a hut (presumably one cohabited by people in cahoots). *Consorts with* means associating with someone in an unsavory manner. • *There is semi-proof that Robin Hood may have already been in cohorts with the Wicked Witch, at the beginning of season 3.*

WILDERTHANWILDE.TUMBLR.COM • 9 JUN 2014

cold slaw

Slaw can be served either *cold* or hot. *Cole*, from the Dutch *kool* (*cabbage*), derives from the same word as *kale*. *Slaw*, from the Dutch *sla* (*salad*), gets its name from salted vegetables. • *Now, if that doesn't get you, how about some of the best ever baked beans, homemade potato salad, homemade cold slaw, and the clincher, homemade ice cream!*

WWW.NCMGCARCLUB.ORG • 10 AUG 2014

collaborating evidence

Corroborating evidence makes a legal case more robust (from

cor-, Latin for *together,* and *roborare,* Latin for *strength*).
Collaborating means working together (*col-* for *again,*
plus *laborare,* Latin for *work*). Collaborators might cor-
roborate each other's alibis, but *evidence* of their collab-
oration would undercut the case. • *The tsunami Butler
modeled had some collaborating evidence revealed at the
same conference in San Francisco.*

WWW.ALASKADISPATCH.COM • 16 MAY 2014

collars, with flying

Usually a PUN on the tradition of *flying colors* (flags) as a sign
of naval triumph. An EGGCORN if it refers to the wing
collars of some men's formal wear or the collars of an avi-
ator's flight suit. • *passed exam 70-298 with flying collars.
Actually I did not have much idea about Designing Security
for a Microsoft Windows Server 2003 Network so I was
very fearful.*

WWW.VELOCITYREVIEWS.COM • 16 MAY 2014

color-coating

Color-coding assigns colors to particular messages (red=*stop,*
green=*go,* yellow=*caution,* etc.). Printers use coding systems to specify certain colors, some of which are for coated
(glossy) paper, and some of which are for matte (non-
glossy) paper. The EGGCORN would color the message,
coating it with color. • *Won't damage the thin pages of your
Bible or scriptures, and with this set, you get four diverse colors,
so making notes/color-coating your Bible study is a breeze!*

REVIEWS.CHRISTIANBOOK.COM • 16 MAY 2014

coma, Oxford

V: *serial coma, lapse into a comma.* Rarely an EGGCORN, often

oxford coma

a PUN, and sometimes a spelling error in which the *o-m-m* of *comma* is heard as that in *commingle* rather than as that in *comment*. An *Oxford coma* might occur after a long lecture, but more probably before the last of a series of three or more such lectures. • *In the case of the Oxford coma, suggest that common sense and style govern its usage.*

WWW.RAGAN.COM • 17 MAY 2014

conjunctive heart failure

Confuses *congestive heart failure* and *congenital heart disease*, and perhaps also the eye condition *conjunctivitis*. Not to be confused with an editor's apoplexy at the lack of a serial comma. • *A person is said to have conjunctive heart failure when the heart can no longer function at a capacity great enough to meet the body's needs.*

BIGHOW.NET •

17 MAY 2014

constellation prize

A common MALA-PROPISM that qualifies as an EGGCORN only if the runners-up get gold stars.

constellation prize

Confused with *consolation prize.* • *Top 10 will all leave with a constellation prize.*

HOUSEPLAYNYC.COM • 17 MAY 2014

copywrite

V: *copy righter.* Writers of commercial text are often called *copy writers*, confused here with *copyright*, federal law that protects intellectual property. Often the copyright on work by copy writers is owned by the company that employs them, not the writers themselves. • *This question is similar to one found on the June 2005 LSAT (section B #1), but has been modified so as to not violate copywrite laws.*

WWW.LAWSCHOOLDISCUSSION.ORG • 17 MAY 2014

cord, touched a

V: *struck a cord, touched a chord, vocal chords.* Confuses the IDIOMS *touched a nerve* and *struck a chord*, the former connoting sensitivity, the latter harmony. Vocal *cords* can produce music; hammers striking piano wires can produce *chords*; and *touching a nerve* is painful. • *Her online plea touched a cord in the nation's heart, bringing a phenomenal viral response.*

WWW.REDORBIT.COM • 15 MAY 2014

cornroll

Confuses the practice of styling hair in rows of tight braids known as *cornrows* with the practice of using hair *rollers*, and possibly with terms such as *egg roll, logroll*, etc. • *Depending upon the style that you request, most cornroll hair styles will take 1 to 3 hours with or without using human/ synthetic hair.*

IMAGEOFAFRICALA.COM • 18 MAY 2014

corporal form

Corporal and *corporeal* are easily confused. *Corporal* things relate to the human body (such as *corporal punishment*) and to a military rank; *corporeal* is STANDARD USAGE for describing our existence as physical (rather than as spiritual) beings. The MALAPROPISM could refer to existence as a (very solid) soldier. • *Some have transcended the corporal form and become an otherworldly being.*

RANDOMHOUSEINDIA.WORDPRESS.COM • 18 MAY 2014

counter with, in

V: *runs counter with, in counter to.* Confuses *in contact with* and *encounter.* The variants garble *in contrast with* and *runs counter to.* • *The student-athlete will learn to lead by example, as well as to learn how communicate with respect to everyone they come in counter with.*

G3LACROSSE.COM • 9 JUN 2014

cove, treasure

Arrr! *Trove* comes from the French *trouver* (*to find*), and a *treasure trove* is literally found treasure. Pirate stories often tell of treasure chests buried in deserted *coves*, which leads to the confusion. • *During this exhibition, the gallery will be transformed into a treasure cove and artist boutique, filled with wearable and one-of-a kind jewelry collections and handcrafted originals!*

BLOG.LIGHTGREYARTLAB.COM • 18 MAY 2014

cow-tow

V: *cow-tail.* Chinese *kētóu* (磕头, *knock-head*) describes a deep, kneeling bow of obeisance called *kowtowing* by

English colonialists. The braid that many Chinese people wore in past centuries might resemble a *cow tail*, but cows aren't *towed* as an act of obeisance, so *cow-tow* is usually just a misspelling. • *First, it is a Christian country that does not cow tow to the Muslims and will not negotiate with them as Obama wants.*

CHRONICLE.AUGUSTA.COM • 18 MAY 2014

crawler, French

Crullers are actually German, not French. A *cruller* (Dutch for *curled*) describes a kind of squarish and twisted cake. However, the version marketed by Dunkin Donuts as a *French Cruller* is round like a

french crawler

donut and resembles the tires of earthmovers—sometimes called *crawlers*. Even so, the MALAPROPISM is usually not an EGGCORN. • *I choose a French Crawler from Dunkin' Donuts. It was awesome.*****

WWW.SPARKPEOPLE.COM • 8 JUN 2014

crutch of the matter

Crux (Latin for *cross*), when taken figuratively to mean a difficulty (where things cross), shares ETYMOLOGY with *crutch*, meaning a crotch, or forked stick. The EGGCORN conveys the sense of a decision point that combines a crossroads and a fork in the road. • *I guess over time it has altered a little but the crutch of the matter is that Percy always looked to gain an edge.*

CAMBRIDGE-FPAS.CO.UK • 18 MAY 2014

cuddlefish

Usually a deliberate PUN or a misspelling. The squidlike *cuttlefish* is slimy, not cuddly, so this is rarely an EGGCORN, except maybe in the case of a stuffed toy cephalopod. • *If I have a cuddlefish ink allergy, does this mean I'm also allergic to Squid and Octopus inks?*

cuddlefish

ANSWERS.YAHOO.COM • 20 MAY 2014

cue, lined up in a

Queue comes from an old French word for *tail*. *Queue* was once a peculiarly British term (named after the long braids worn by sailors and others, also spelled *cue*) for a line of people. Increasingly, it is part of American English, too. In American usage *cue* usually refers to a stick used in billiards. • *Considering that 42 photographers, most with DryZone camera bags were lined up in a cue for check-in, we sort of stood out from the crowd.*

WWW.PHOTOSHOPNEWS.COM • 18 MAY 2014

curtsey call

curtsey call

A *courtesy call* might refer to an official visit by a diplomat or to a phone call. The EGGCORN suggests a visitor *curtseying* to a host. A *courtesy* is the old-fashioned word for a *curtsy* or *curtsey*, and female per-

formers often curtsy during a *curtain call* after a show. •
*On August 20, 2009, Madam Vivienne Yeda Apopo, Director
General of the East African Development Bank, paid a curt-
sey call to the Ministry of Foreign Affairs and Cooperation.*

WWW.MINAFFET.GOV.RW • 18 MAY 2014

curve (your) enthusiasm

V: *curve (your) appetite. Curb* was originally *curve*, and the
EGGCORN brings this expression back to its roots. A *curb*
was a *curved* restraining strap attached to a horse's bit.
The change from the standard *curb (your) enthusiasm* appears to refer to a graph in which the line of enthusiasm
bends downward. • *To help me curve my enthusiasm, I have
been planning my little heart out.*

WWW.FACEBOOK.COM • 10 AUG 2014

damper (your enthusiasm, etc.)

Confuses the phrases *dampens your enthusiasm* with *temper
your enthusiasm*, or perhaps with TAMP DOWN ON. A flue's
damper regulates a fire's heat, while *tempering* metal hard-
ens and strengthens it. Perhaps *dampering* enthusiasm
or anger also restricts heat. • *An injury may have kept
15-year-old Maggie Voisin from competing in Sochi, but it did
nothing to damper the enthusiasm of her hometown crowd.*

MTPR.ORG • 20 MAY 2014

darn right

Downright (as in *downright scary*) is a COLLOQUIAL attributive used to intensify another adjective. The EGGCORN *darn right* combines the euphemism *darn* with another colloquial attributive, *right* (meaning *very*), and confuses them with *downright*. • *Although uncomfortable (or darn right painful), the vast majority of cases of back pain should not be considered a medical emergency.*

WWW.BURLINGTONNATURALHEALTH.CA • 20 MAY 2014

dashboard stomach

dashboard stomach

Washboards are rare these days, but *dashboards* are plentiful—many constructed of smooth, sculpted polyurethane. Still, a steering wheel would be hard to fit under your shirt. • *If you are not blessed with a dashboard stomach, your best hope is doing the right stomach toning exercises.*

WWW.FITNESSHEALTHZONE.COM • 20 MAY 2014

dawn (a hat, etc.)

V: *don on (someone), dong on (someone)*. *Donning* and *doffing* are antique in today's mostly hatless fashion world, so a writer might extend the METAPHOR of an idea *dawning* to putting on clothes. *Dong* might refer to something that *rings a bell*. • *So, after dinner, he dawned his coat and boots and let himself out through the oversized doors of the entrance hall.*

LIVETHEMAGIC.FORUMOTION.ORG • 22 MAY 2014

day, up to

Confuses *day* and *date*, perhaps influenced by *day planners* and *day-at-a-glance* calendars. • *They also keep me up to day on things that are coming up that will be needing attention.*

WWW.CBAC.COM • 22 MAY 2014

death charge

Antisubmarine *depth charges* are certainly deadly, so the EGG-CORN makes sense. Murder allegations against sailors who deploy them are unlikely. • *"We saw one submarine but he took off," Wilson recalled. "We dropped death charges. After, they'd have their torpedoes shoot up. One of them was full of garbage to make it look like they'd been shot."*

WWW.BANNERGRAPHIC.COM • 22 MAY 2014

decease, cease and

Decease's ETYMOLOGY (from *dēcessus,* Latin for *departure*) concerns death in the sense of *going away,* not stopping. It gets mixed up with the legal threat and demand to *cease and desist,* which means *stop, and don't do it again.* A *cease and decease* letter probably isn't actually demanding your death. • *In September 2005, we send a "Cease and Decease" letter to what was then a distributor of our product line.*

WWW.JUSTANSWER.COM • 22 MAY 2014

deep-seeded

The METAPHOR *deep-seated* (meaning *firmly established*) comes from an old use of the word *seat* that meant a *foundation* that made for a sturdier building. The MALA-PROPISM *deep-seeded* confuses it with *deep-rooted*; its METAPHOR of deeply buried seeds that sprout actually makes sense when it describes repressed feelings. • *I've outlined a series of questions that I often pose to clients as we work through the process of unearthing and confronting those deep seeded feelings.*

LASINGLESSOCIETY.COM • 24 MAY 2014

deformation of character

Fame originally meant *rumor,* and *defamation of character* is a legal term that means spreading bad rumors about someone. Unanswered, such libel and slander can make one's character seem ugly (or *deformed*). • *Dominica's prime minister wants compensation from US based economist for deformation of character.*

DOMINICAVIBES.DM • 24 MAY 2014

defunked

Defunct means dead—no longer *functional.* You could argue that a band without *funk* is as good as dead, too, which might explain the mistake. • *Yuka Honda and Miho played in the band "Butter 08" as a side project. . . . The now defunked "Butter 08" is legendary among the Cibo Matto family.*

WWW.DAMOON.NET • 24 MAY 2014

de la Rosa, Via

Via Dolorosa (*Way of Sorrows*) is said to be the Jerusalem street that Jesus walked to his Crucifixion. *Via de la Rosa* would be the *Street of the Rose.* But since the rose is a METAPHOR for the Virgin Mary, and many famous works of art depict *Maria Dolorosa* (*Mary of the Sorrows*) mourning Jesus's death, this could qualify as an EGGCORN. • *The Via De La Rosa is the road that winds through old Jeru-*

salem, and according to legend, is the place where Jesus began his walk. . . .

WWW.ANDYBRANER.TYPEPAD.COM • 30 JUL 2014

demure, to

Demure people are shy and modest, and might modestly *demur* (raise objections) if asked to speak their minds; but they can't *demure*—it isn't a verb. • *I would demure from shaking hands with visiting business associates. "Sorry, I have a skin condition. Don't worry. It's not contagious."*

WWW.INSPIRE.COM • 24 MAY 2014

despite (your) face, cut off (your) nose

The saying *cut off your nose to spite your face* deplores pointlessly self-defeating behavior. The word *spite* actually developed from *despite*, so the antique form of the saying would have been *cutting off your nose in despite of your face*, which gives the EGGCORN an ancient pedigree. But *despite* has taken on the meaning *even though* or *without regard to*, so the MALAPROPISM seems to describe rhinoplasty without regard to appearance, which may explain certain nose jobs in Hollywood. • *We're all doing fine, financially. There's no reason to cut off your nose despite your face just to prove that you're worth it.*

COLLIDER.COM • 25 MAY 2014

desserts, just

Dessert comes from the Latin *dis-servir* (*un-serve*), a dish at the end of the meal after the table had been un-served, or cleared. Those origins differ from those of the Latin *dēservīre* (*to serve well*), which gives us *deserve* and *just deserts* (*proper rewards*). However, since most of us have

just desserts

been brought up to believe that if you've been good, you get to eat dessert, the EGGCORN *just desserts* makes sense, too. • *Press Clips: Lara Logan Gets Her Just Desserts.*

WWW.CALBUZZ.COM • 27 JUN 2014

diarrhetic

Confuses two similar-sounding words. Number 1: *diuretic*, a medicine that causes one's body to get rid of fluids through urination. Number 2: *diarrhea*, a liquid discharge of the bowels; there is an uncommon form of the adjective *diarrheic* that's spelled *diarrhetic*. People often find mistakes involving Number 2 to be funny. • *One of the key points hilighted about alcolohol is its diarrhetic effects and hence how it dehydrates you.*

WWW.ABC.NET.AU • 28 MAY 2014

die-hearted

Confuses *die-hard* with expressions such as *big-hearted, noble-hearted*, etc. *Diehards* may fight to the end, but their hearts are set on surviving, not dying. • *We are die-hearted like Usain Bolt and our other great Jamaican athletes, so we are there to do our best and represent Jamaica.*

JAMAICA-GLEANER.COM • 26 MAY 2014

died in the wool

Dyed in the wool refers not to wool from dead sheep, but wool *dyed* (colored) before it is spun, a process that makes the colors more durable. It is a METAPHOR for deeply held beliefs. • *To be a certified, died in the wool lefty you MUST always toe the party line, even when you know it to be wrong.*

FIVETHIRTYEIGHT.COM • 26 MAY 2014

diffuse (a bomb, etc.)

The action of particles spreading in air or water is known as *diffusion*, but the verb *diffuse* is often confused with *disperse* (go in different directions) and *defuse* (remove a fuse). You could *diffuse tension* (dispersing it over a wide area) by *defusing the quarrel* (removing the explosive trigger). • *Quick thinking when there's bombs around is never easy (have you ever seen anyone in a movie diffuse a bomb without thinking about it for at least a minute?)*

WWW.CANDYCRUSH-LEVEL.COM • 26 MAY 2014

disguard

Discard (to get rid of something) may or may not have originated from card games. However, it never meant *letting your guard down* or removing protections from something, which the EGGCORN suggests. • *Choose your favorite disguarded greeting cards from thousands of available designs.*

FINEARTAMERICA.COM • 26 MAY 2014

disingenuine

V: *disungenuine*. This sounds like a word coined by Yogi Berra. It combines *disingenuous* (tricky) and *in/un-genuine* (fake) to create what linguist Arnold Zwicky identifies as a PORTMANTEAU word. • *How disingenuine to fool your own fans into reading your article this way . . . shame on you sir.*

JOELCOMM.COM • 27 MAY 2014

dissolutioned

Confuses *dissolute* (lacking morals) with *disillusioned* (losing one's illusions), and possibly with the lack of *solutions*, or of solids precipitating from a liquid. It's certainly possible to be disillusioned when the truth about a dissolute person comes out in the wash. • *Of Course, Neo Conservatives are all ex-liberals dissolutioned by reality.*

BOATERTALK.COM • 26 MAY 2014

diswrought

Confuses *distraught* with *overwrought* or *wrought up*. *Distraught* means *distracted* in the sense of *driven crazy*. *Overwrought* means *worked too hard* in the sense of metal beaten by a blacksmith until it becomes brittle. *Wrought up* means *stirred up*. The EGGCORN combines them to convey the sense of being upset. • *She is very diswrought about the whole thing and this makes her hate computers even more.*

ANSWERS.YAHOO.COM • 27 MAY 2014

do diligence

V: *do process, do to the fact, give him his do, give credit where credit is do*. Replaces an adjective, *due* (the legal steps of diligence that are required), with a verb, *do* (taking action on those steps). This HOMOPHONE leads to many *due/do* MALAPROPISMS because of the vague association between needing to *do* something and the date on which it is *due*. • *Don't do your do diligence two weeks before the sale. Wait until at least one week before the sale.*

WWW.TAXLIENLADY.COM • 28 MAY 2014

doggy-dog

V: *doggy-dog world.* Usually a PUN, but in a world where canines find their ways into many IDIOMS, the confusion with a *dog-eat-dog world* isn't surprising. Interestingly, according to the *OED*, the Latin original for that saying (from 42 B.C.E.) was that *dog does not eat dog.* So maybe it is *a doggy-dog world*, after all. • *We urge people to use REALTORS because of our Code of Ethics . . . but many fail to realize that real estate today is a doggy dog world and they forget a couple of things.*

ACTIVERAIN.TRULIA.COM • 28 MAY 2014

dough-eyed

It's tempting to speculate that the fairly recent term *doe-eyed* (meaning a look that is soft, feminine, and perhaps somewhat blankly naive) may have been an EGGCORN itself, deriving from *dew* or *dewy.* Those who use the modern MALAPROPISM may instead envision Poppin' Fresh, the Pillsbury Doughboy. • *At no point do you care if these dough-eyed buffoons live or die.*

WWW.IGN.COM • 28 MAY 2014

dramatic experience

V: *childhood drama. Drama* and *trauma* both come from classical Greek words, but trauma meant a wound, and drama a tragic play. Which is not to say that trauma isn't dramatic or that drama can't be traumatic. • *I started my desire to lose weight after I went through a dramatic experience with my family causing me to gain weight.*

WWW.MYFITNESSPAL.COM • 30 MAY 2014

duct tape

duct tape

Yes, *duct tape* was an EGGCORN and MALAPROPISM, though now it's the STANDARD USAGE. The name came from strips of *duck* fabric (untwilled canvas or denim named from the Dutch *doeck*, or linen cloth). Rubberized duck tape worked well for duct work and became known in the 1950s as *duct tape*. To bring things full circle, one company now brands its product Duck Tape. • *It's DUCT tape, not DUCK tape! Ducks have nothing to do with this tape!!!*

WWW.FACEBOOK.COM • 27 JUN 2014

due, make

V: *make dew, mind due. Making do* occurs when the *rent is due*, the *phone bill is due*, etc., which may influence the EGGCORN *making due*. But then it might also be an expedient of librarians stamping books as they check them out.

due or die

The variant *mind due* (for *mind you*) suggests a *due date* on memories. • *Sometimes you just have to make due with what you have.*

WWW.LIFEASAMORTICIANS WIFE.COM • 5 JUL 2014

due or die

Probably inspired by

deadlines rather than by irate librarians. The medieval Scottish motto *do or die* referred to a hero's resolution to perform a deed or die trying. • *The cold hard truth facing the Blues players and Ken Hitchcock today is that its due or die time.*

WWW.HOCKEYBUZZ.COM • 30 MAY 2014

dungeon, high

Many *dungeons* were in fact high. *Dungeon*, or *donjon*, referred to the central keep (or tower) of a medieval castle, which sometimes served as a prison. *Dudgeon* means anger, though no one is quite sure where the word comes from. *High*

high dungeon

dudgeon (outrage) might have landed you in the dungeon if expressed to the face of the medieval lord of the castle. • *We criticise her because she is totally out of her depth, basically a stupid woman with her hyperbowl and high dungeon (among others).*

ANNESUMMERS.COM.AU • 30 MAY 2014

dye is cast, the

The die is cast was originally said in Latin by Caesar upon his crossing the Rubicon, and it refers to tossing dice in the sense that *it's in fate's hands now*. Some assume that the expression means the making of a *die* for the forging of tools—an object that, once cast, can't be easily changed.

Furthermore, once *dye* is cast into a liquid and then colors what's soaking there, it's too late to change. So all three versions, taken figuratively, mean essentially the same thing. • *The leaf, flower or fruit color you see isn't always the color you get when the dye is cast.*

WWW.THESTATE.COM • 31 MAY 2014

each's own, to

There's no neuter singular personal pronoun in English, which leads to interesting gymnastics by writers attempting to avoid such gendering expressions as *to each his own*. This phrase is an example of that, as the EGGCORN is neither masculine, nor feminine, nor correct. • *I was a little thrown off by the sign for Holy Yoga outside. To each's own, I guess.*

WWW.YELP.COM • 31 MAY 2014

eardrop on

V: *ease drop on. Eavesdrop* originally described the space (the eavesdrop) close to a house where water dripped from the eaves of the roof—and where one's *ears* might catch conversations within. The EGGCORN uses *drop* as a verb, perhaps in the sense of *dropping in* to be near enough to hear easily. • *It was rude to eardrop on them so I don't know what they were talking about.*

HANDBALL123.COM • 31 MAY 2014

earshout, within

Unlike EAVESDROP, *earshot* never became a verb; we don't talk about *earshooting* someone. *Earshot* dates from the 1600s as an analogue of *bowshot*, meaning *within hearing range*, so *within earshout* makes perfect EGGCORN-ish nonsense. • *Not normally a comedian, he got a chuckle out of everyone within earshout.*

WWW.STLSOCCER.NET • 1 JUN 2014

eau claire, chocolate

V: *chocolate eggclair.* The French *éclair* alludes to a flash of lightning, presumably because of the speed with which the pastry is consumed. The recipe—whether for a *chocolate eggclair* or an *eau claire* made by Wisconsin chefs—doesn't call for any *eggs* at all in the choux pastry; however, the cream or custard filling can be very eggy indeed. • *I had a couple of macarons, espresso and an aaaammazzing mango mousse pastry. Joel had an espresso and chocolate eau claire.*

KITTYCOTTEN.COM • 1 JUN 2014

egg corn

V: *egg-corn, eggcorn.* The story of how the first EGGCORN gave its name to a whole category of peculiarly modern MALAPROP-ISMS is told in the introduction to this dictionary, on page 1. • *Squirrels feast on pine cones, bird seed, egg corns, walnuts, and during Halloween pumpkins.*

egg corn

WWW.MIBATCONTROL.COM • 1 JUN 2014

eggtopic pregnancy

Confuses the serious condition known as *ectopic pregnancy*, when the fertilized *egg* implants outside the uterus. *Ectopic* comes from the Latin *ectopia*, which means *out of place*. • *Normally, but not always you have pain in your shoulders with an eggtopic pregnancy.*

WWW.CIRCLEOFMOMS.COM • 1 JUN 2014

elementary canal

Confuses the uncommon word *aliment* (something that nourishes) with the more common word *element* (something that's basic). The confusion doesn't explain why children in *elementary* school are so fascinated by the workings of the *alimentary canal*. • *It is the opinion of doctors that treat arthritic patients with saponins that the saponins reduce the production of inflammatory toxins in the elementary canal.*

elementary canal

WWW.SAPONINS.COM • 2 JUN 2014

elk

The archaic *ilk* (which basically meant *like*, but was spelled inside out) adds a touch of literary snootiness to your vocabulary if used conventionally. Used unconventionally, as by the writer below and his ilk, mistakenly alluding to the noble species *Cervus canadensis*, it permits others to be snooty. Usually just a MALAPROPISM, it might be an EGG-

CORN if used in the sense of a reference to someone's *herd*.
• *I wish I could get a handle on why he and his elk are winning.*

FORUMS.RANDI.ORG • 2 JUN 2014

empirical (grandeur, majesty, etc.)

Confuses the grandeur of *empire* with the elegance of evidence that is *empirical* (from the Latin for *medicine,* or *remedy*). Usually a simple MALAPROPISM or misspelling rather than an EGGCORN. • *Blessed be Most High. His Empirical Majesty Haile Selassie II. The true Lion of Judah from the House of Solomon.*

WWW.TRIBALWAR.COM • 6 JUN 2014

enact revenge on

V: *enact vengeance on, extract punishment on*, etc. Confuses *an act of revenge* with the STANDARD USAGE, *exact revenge* (literally to *drive out* revenge). All of the variants, though defensible, misconstrue the phrase, which means forcing a payment of retribution from unwilling people. • *I should enact revenge on him by treating him like an infant when he confuses Java and JavaScript!*

ALPHA.APP.NET • 2 JUN 2014

end, from here on

Confuses IDIOMS such as *from beginning to end* or *for weeks on end* with the usual *from here on in* (from now on). • *From here on end it's about freedom and owning your life again.*

WWW.YTRAVELBLOG.COM • 3 JUN 2014

enlarge, by

V: *by in large*. The nautical term *by and large*, which sums up the entirety of a ship's sailing characteristics, came to mean *on the whole*. So *enlarging* the whole picture makes some sense. • *The staff by enlarge were great although we did find the reception staff a little less obliging than we had become used to in Thailand.*

WWW.TRIPADVISOR.COM • 12 MAY 2014

escape goat

escape goat

V: *scrapegoat.* A *scapegoat* allowed the ancient Israelites to *escape* their sins. Leviticus 16 instructs the priest to lay the people's sins upon a goat and send it into the wilderness, a rite that might get the sinner out of many a moral scrape. • *"By using the word of 'sacked' they made me an escape goat" said Sajid.*

GROUPS.GOOGLE.COM • 3 JUN 2014

eurologist

Usually just a misspelling rather than a reference to *European* doctors of *urology*, but it raises an interesting question: If a PhD who teaches American literature is an Americanist, would a PhD who teaches European literature be a *Eurologist*? • *This problem that has been bothering me since jan of 09 and every eurologist, dermatologist and dr have told me its not an std by any means.*

WWW.OURHEALTH.COM • 3 JUN 2014

evasive surgery

Might describe mobsters getting plastic surgery to change their appearances, but usually just a MALAPROPISM confusing *elective surgery* (not medically necessary) with *invasive surgery* (that goes deep into the body). • *New technology, procedures and equipment allow our staff to use minimally-evasive surgery to place pins, wires, screws, and plates on the bone to stabilize it.*

WWW.HOSURGERY.COM • 3 JUN 2014

exercise (your) demons

One sense of *exercise* is to worry or perplex someone, which could help this MALAPROPISM qualify as an EGGCORN. Demons about to be *exorcised* (cast out) would understandably be *exercised* about the process. • *I write so I can (a) exercise my demons, (b) breathe, and (c) entertain fantasies about becoming rich and famous.*

WWW.MANICMUMBLING.COM • 3 JUN 2014

exorcised over, to become

Unlike the previous entry, this is clearly an EGGCORN, conveying the idea that one might get *exercised* (upset) enough to "raise hell"—and perhaps cast out demons. • *All that said, it's not as easy to become exorcised over the Terps' exclusion as I thought.*

VOICES.WASHINGTONPOST.COM • 3 JUN 2014

expatriot

An *ex-patriot* (someone formerly patriotic) need not be an *expatriate* (citizen living abroad). Still, one might reasonably doubt that a true patriot would live abroad, so this qualifies as an EGGCORN. • *It is my understanding that when having expatriot status you are allowed back into the states a maximum of 65 days per year.*

DR1.COM • 3 JUN 2014

explanation point

V: *explanation mark*. Combining the *exclamation* and an *explanation*, this could be the proper punctuation for humorist Ring Lardner's famous sentence, "'Shut up,' he explained." The near-HOMOPHONE contributes to a mix-up between *explaining* (literally, *flattening out* so that it can be understood) and *exclaiming* (calling out). • *When I try to open iTunes on my PC a dialog box comes up with the yellow triangle containing an explanation point.*

DISCUSSIONS.APPLE.COM • 3 JUN 2014

explicative deleted

Confuses *expletive* (a cussword), *explication* (analysis), and possibly *explicit*. Something that's *explicative* explains things. An *explicative expletive* might be something like "damnfool," which a censorious EGGCORN-writer would delete as too *explicit*. • *Big Papi is home in his (explicative deleted) city he wouldn't be the same somewhere else.*

WWW.PATRIOTLEDGER.COM • 3 JUN 2014

expotential growth

Confuses *growth potential* and *exponential growth*, both of which are phrases of pseudoscientific jargon meant to lure money or talent to speculative enterprises. Many failed ventures of that sort show *ex-potential*. • *Due to expotential growth, I am looking for three talented, varying level of exp. Software Development Engineers.*

WWW.LINKEDIN.COM • 4 JUN 2014

expresso, cup of

Confuses *express* (*special* or *fast*) with the Italian *espresso* (*from the press*), a steam-brewed coffee that produces a quick caffeine buzz. "Expresso Love," a song by the rock group Dire Straits, punned on caffeinated romance. • *[W]e take care of our coffee right up to the final cup of expresso, in order to guarantee the end user a total Caffè River experience.*

WWW.CAFFERIVER.COM • 3 JUN 2014

exuberant prices

Former Federal Reserve Board Chair Alan Greenspan's famous warning of "irrational exuberance" in the economy may have inspired this confusion of *exuberant* (energetic, super-fertile) with *exorbitant* (high-priced, beyond the usual track), two words that connote excess. • *Retail investors are always too late to the party and way too excited to pay exuberant prices for highly speculative stocks.*

WWW.INVESTWITHALEX.COM • 4 JUN 2014

far-gone conclusion

Confuses distance and time. A *foregone conclusion* is reached *before* the question is even asked; *far gone* refers to something that is far away or has deteriorated (*too far gone*). Referring to the past in terms of distance (*distant past*, a time *long past*) adds to the confusion. • *Now I'm certainly not saying it's a far gone conclusion that young Brandon Harris is going to be the starting QB for the Tigers.*

WWW.WWL.COM • 4 JUN 2014

fartlick

All sniggering aside, this MALAPROPISM isn't an EGGCORN unless the writer in question thinks that exercise makes one savor disgusting odors. The Swedish term *fartlek* translates as *speed play* and describes an interval training method for athletes. • *[M]ake one of these runs a 'fart lick' run. That means that you run one minute slow, one minute fast, two minutes slow, two minutes fast, three minutes slow, three minutes fast.*

WWW.MADEMAN.COM • 4 JUN 2014

fast majority

fast majority

V: *fast swathes*, *fast tracts*, etc. *Fast* and *vast* are adjectives that sound alike. A *fast majority* might suggest not only a majority reached quickly but also one that's *firmly fixed* or *steady*—one that resembles a *vast* (wide, or large) majority. • *The fast majority of our customers also use a small amount of data.*

WWW.DSLREPORTS.COM • 4 MAY 2014

fate accompli

A *fait accompli* is an *accomplished fact*, but what sometimes seems like *fate*'s doing is usually the work of people who have already arranged what will happen—so the mix-up is both an easy one to make and a common EGGCORN. • *Many borrowers accept this reality as a fate accompli, and do not even bother to read their loan documents in any detail.*

feeble position, curled up in a

An unborn child in a *fetal position* seems weak and helpless, which explains the confusion here. The two words also share some sexist cultural and literary associations: *Feeble* (weak) originates from a Latin word for something *to be wept over*; *fetal* (relating to a fetus) originates from the same preliterate Indo-European word that gives us *female.* • *She was deep into her thoughts, crouched into a corner, while in the feeble position.*

feeble position

ferment trouble

v: *ferment fears*, *ferment unrest*, etc. A *fomentation* was originally a warm bath or compress that encouraged healing, and to *foment trouble* came to mean to *encourage trouble*. The bacterial process of *fermentation* also generates heat, and *ferment* came to be used as a verb (to brew) and a noun (agitation). One could actually *foment ferment.* • *Of particular concern to the Indian government, are channels that ferment trouble and threaten national integrity.*

felt a fission

fission, felt a

The temperature at the core of a nuclear *fission* explosion is estimated at 100 million degrees kelvin, so it would feel hot. *Frisson*, by way of contrast, is French for *shiver* and derives from the Latin *frigere* (*to be cold*). Of course, when two people feel a frisson, it can run both hot and cold. • *She looked so goddamned beautiful standing there, and he felt a fission of desire sweep through him, God! He had missed her.*

WWW.WATTPAD.COM • 5 JUN 2014

flamingo dance

flamingo dance

Spanish *flamenco*, which describes the traditional dance with its dramatic poses, actually means *flamingo*, the bird the dance is named after. The EGGCORN thus returns the word to its origin. • *I am going to Spain and wanted to know what city has Flamingo Dance Shows that I can go to.*

ANSWERS.YAHOO.COM • 4 JUN 2014

flare for (the dramatic, etc.)

A *flare* shines or burns brightly, to get attention, which may explain why it gets confused with the *flair* that connotes personal style. *Flair* actually comes from a French word for a distinctive scent, so someone with a *flair for the dra-*

matic (a talent for comedy, perhaps) could smell funny. • *She helped me use my flare for the dramatic as an advantage not an impairment—by casting me as the female leading role in our class.*

IMPACT.WEBERSHANDWICK.COM • 5 JUN 2014

flaw in the ointment

Ecclesiastes 10:1 observes that "[d]ead flies make the perfumer's ointment give off a foul odour." This is the source of *fly in the ointment*, an expression that shows how a small irritant can spoil everything. It's confused with a *flaw*—a small, irritating problem. • *The only flaw in the ointment was that when I contracted MRSA, I was put in isolation and the hospital was being redecorated.*

WWW.RATEMYHOSPITAL.IE • 5 JUN 2014

floundered, the boat

A *flounder*, which lives in water, flops awkwardly on land and may have gotten its name from an old Dutch word for flopping about in a mire—or vice versa. The verb *founder*, which comes from molten metal (as in a *foundry*) bursting through the bottom of a mold, came to describe leaky ships that were *foundering*, or taking on water before sinking. • *In 1980, sixteen Danish fishermen were forced to jump into the North Sea after their fishing boat floundered.*

REBUILDINGCIVILIZATION.COM • 5 JUN 2014

flush (something) out

V: *flesh against.* Instead of *fleshing out* a bare-bones idea, one might *flush it out* as quail are flushed from cover—or as a flush of shame fills a face, though perhaps not as a toilet is flushed. But you wouldn't push your chair *flesh against* the wall. • *Overall I don't like this song but I don't hate it either. With some work and the idea flushed out it could be good.*

WWW.ULTIMATE-GUITAR.COM • 5 JUN 2014

foolhearty

V: *fullhardy.* Some fools are *hardy,* some are *hearty,* and they're easily confused HOMOPHONES. *Hardy* traditionally meant tough and daring; someone who was foolishly daring was *foolhardy. Hearty* just means strong and cheerful. The quality of *foolhardiness* is unmistakable. • *It is really fool hearty to invite further loss from the Democrats.*

WWW.DEMOCRATICUNDERGROUND.COM • 6 JUN 2014

for, far be it

Linguist Arnold Zwicky suggests that this may be "a blend of '*far be it from [me to say]*' and '*it's not for [me to say].*'" *Far . . . from* would be the STANDARD USAGE, not *far . . . for.* • *Far be it for me to say if any of those apply to me but even if they don't I'm certainly not going to shatter any illusions.*

SPENCERMATTHEWSMALEONLINE.DAILYMAIL.CO.UK • 7 JUN 2014

forward, wrote a

The front of a ship is *forward;* a *foreword* often precedes a book's text. Both are in front, but only one is made of words. The HOMOPHONES nevertheless leave a lot of writers at sea as to which is which. • *The book was published by Stone Edge Farm, a Sonoma wine estate whose owner, Mac McQuown, wrote the book's forward.*

WWW.PRESSDEMOCRAT.COM • 7 JUN 2014

fowl swoop, one

V: *one foul swoop. Fell* (from the same root that gives us *felon*) means *murderous and violent.* Shakespeare's Macduff seems to have envisioned Macbeth as a chicken hawk, swooping down on the flock with evil intent, when he bewailed the *foul* (immoral) murder of his wife and children— "all my pretty chickens

one fowl swoop

and their dam,/ At *one fell swoop*," so *swooping fowls* are certainly relevant. In this case, the chickens come before the EGGCORNS. • *We will be in and done—in one fowl swoop. You will get to watch a beautifully landscaped garden unfold daily before your eyes.*

WWW.GARDENOFEDENLANDSCAPES.COM • 25 SEPT 2014

French benefits

Many employed in France enjoy generous *fringe benefits*, such as a month of paid vacation, but the French model of compensation has not become a byword in the USA. It has, however, become an EGGCORN, if a rare one. • *Hopefully they'll be able to keep their French benefits through the end of the month.*

FORUMS.FOOTBALLGUYS.COM • 8 JUN 2014

front in center

Front and center! is a military command. It orders someone in drill formation to leave the protection of the ranks and move to the front and center. One could say this means putting one's *front in (the) center*, conveying the sense of taking a prominent position. • *[I]n the final push before Tuesday's election, schools are now front in center in the race.*

SFAPPEAL.COM • 8 JUN 2014

fullproof

Confuses *foolproof* with phrases such as *fully proof against, fully protected, fully secure*, etc. • *4 Full-Proof Ways To Get Over Your Ex Before Valentine's Day.*

WWW.MENSXP.COM • 8 JUN 2014

furl your brow

Old-fashioned square-rigged sails, when *furled* (folded, gathered, and tied horizontally along a boom) the traditional way, actually do resemble the creases of a *furrowed brow*, so this goof is logical. Modern, roller-furled sails (rolled up smoothly like roller blinds) would be a good META-PHOR only for a Botoxed forehead. • *Thoughts of some of those tough times may make you furl your brow.*

THELEADERSLOCKER.COM • 8 JUN 2014

futile lords

Seen from today, the petty warring of medieval nobles certainly seems *futile*—a time when might made right and literacy was rare. But scholars who've studied the so-called *feudal* system say the reasons for medieval conflicts were more logical than most people believe. • *Many of them practiced democracy while Europe was ruled buy kings and futile lords.*

PARNELLHISTORY.WORDPRESS.COM • 8 JUN 2014

g

gain, zero-sum

V: *zero sun game.* A *zero-sum game* is sometimes confused with *no net gain.* Game theory describes a zero-sum game in which the more the winners win, the more the losers lose; winning such a game could thus be called a *zero-sum gain.* (A nighttime baseball contest might be a *zero-sun game.*) • *I am hopeful over the long term, and think the net result will be a zero sum gain.*

WWW.COLLABORATIVE.COM • 9 JUN 2014

gambit, run the

V: *run the gamete. Running the gamut* means playing the entire range of notes on a musical scale. A *gambit,* originally a chess term, is a strategic move. A complex gambit could run the gamut of all possible strategic options. A *gamete* is a haploid (half) cell that joins another to create a fertilized egg—but not an EGGCORN. • *These photos from today run the gambit from super boring and generic to less boring and original.*

HOTHOUSEMONKEY.COM • 9 JUN 2014

gameful employment

You could be *gainfully employed* (in a job that paid real money) by a computer-*game* maker or a casino. *Gameful,* however, is usually just a simple MALAPROPISM. • *On November 20th I will be leaving the Boeing Company so I am looking for other opportunities, otherwise known as gameful employment.*

GROUPS.YAHOO.COM • 9 JUN 2014

gamut between, run the

V: *run the gambit between.* Confuses *running the gamut* (playing all the notes in a scale) and *running the gauntlet between* (enduring an ordeal). The latter comes from a tradition of punishment that forced a soldier to run between two lines of men whacking him with sticks. • *Likewise* Sesame Street *had to run the gamut between corporations, funding entities, educational critics, artists . . . and other people who wanted a show to reflect an all inclusiveness never before seen on the airwaves.*

BLOGS.SLJ.COM • 20 JUN 2014

garbledygook

The *OED* says the word *gobbledygook* probably comes from the sound of a turkey's gobble. It's used to characterize complex, bureaucratic language that results in *garbled* understanding on the part of readers. • *Don't let garbledygook scare you off from a brilliant blogging career, dear writer.*

PLUS.GOOGLE.COM • 9 JUN 2014

gecko, from the

Rare, and a MALAPROPISM that may derive from the ubiquitous talking *gecko* lizard in televised insurance commercials. *Get-go* (or *git-go*) was mid-twentieth-century African-American SLANG for *the start—the get-up-and-go*; it's no longer considered slang. • *He lies to you straight*

from the gecko. Some-
one that lies right away
obviously has no inten-
tion of being with you
forever.

from the gecko

DEEDERS84.HUBPAGES
.COM • 9 JUN 2014

gentile warts

The sexually transmitted
human papillomavi-
rus (HPV) causes *genital warts* on Gentiles and Jews
alike. *Gentile* (a term used for several Hebrew words that
meant *of the races*) has the same origins as *genital* (relating
to sexual organs, from the Latin word for *begetting*). Historically, ritual cleanness distinguished Jew from Gentile,
a symbol of which was circumcision—surgical removal of
the foreskin in male Jews. • *He has gentile warts and now I*
have just been diagnosed with hpv virus.

GENITAL-WARTS.HEALTH-CURES.COM • 10 JUN 2014

get your dandruff up

V: *get your gander up.* The *OED* speculates that *dander* (temper) and *dandruff* (scalp flakes) have related origins.
Therefore, to *get your dander up* (to become agitated)
might derive from hairs standing up on the scalp. The
variant makes some sense, as angry *ganders* may *nip one*
in the BUTT. • *Before you get your dandruff up, listen to my*
logic.

WWW.RAMSONDEMAND.COM • 10 JUN 2014

ghost, gets (your)

Get (your) goat is American SLANG of unknown origin that became current around the beginning of the twentieth century to describe aggravation—perhaps a nod to the goatish Pan, god of wildness. Aggravation might make one feel haunted by spiritual upset. • *Gosh this kind of post really gets my ghost, I live in a country where as a non-national I am not entitled to free health care.*

BABYANDBUMP.MOMTASTIC.COM • 10 JUN 2014

gigacounter

V: *gyga counter. Giga,* from the Greek word for *giant,* commonly denotes a lot of computer data (bytes measured 2^{30}). The *Geiger counter* is named after physicist Hans Geiger, not some absurdly large number that the device calculates as it measures radiation. • *For reference, the clicking sound you hear is the giga counter inside the TV.*

WWW.QUARTERTOTHREE.COM • 9 JUN 2014

girdle your loins

"Gird up thy loins . . . and go thy way," says the prophet Elisha (2 Kings 4:29) to his servant, entrusting him with a holy errand. *Gird* is an antique English word that can mean *girdling* (belting) or, as in the line from the King James Bible, "hitch up your pants and go." Confusion with a woman's undergarment makes this EGGCORN funnier to us than it would have been a century earlier. • *The evenings are drawing in, but it's time once again to girdle your loins and brave the weather for an evening at the National Geographic on Regent Street.*

NATGEOADVENTURE.TV • 10 JUN 2014

Gnome Project, Human

A common misspelling of *genome* rather than an EGGCORN— though it's tempting to imagine research into the DNA codes that reveals why some humans look *gnomish* and others look *elfin.* • *Svante Paabo of the Max Plank institute*

human gnome project

who worked on both the Human gnome project and the Neanderthal gnome project has completed the Neanderthal gnome from fragments drilled out of bones. . . .

THELOOKILOVE.TUMBLR.COM • 15 JUN 2014

goal standard

Confuses *goal* with the METAPHOR of a *gold standard.* The latter comes from the monetary system by which a nation's currency is based on gold holdings that make it "good as gold." Business jargon sometimes uses *goal standard* literally to describe targets, but its metaphorical usage is usually either a PUN about soccer or hockey, or it's an EGGCORN. • *MRI is considered the goal standard image because of its sensitivity and detail.*

WWW.DMANDELMD.COM • 10 JUN 2014

goat, give up the

Confuses the alliterative pairs *gets (his) goat* with *gives up the ghost* and sometimes with the sense of *gives up the ship.* Relinquishing one's ghost, or spirit, might be associated with the ritual sacrifice of a goat. • *Between the spit and the teeth scraping, most base coats give up the goat there, so the tops of my manicures are usually the first places to show chipping.*

LABBUNNY.COM • 10 JUN 2014

granite, take for

Often a deliberate PUN. When something's *taken for granted*, it's a gift (a *grant*) that doesn't require proving. *Granite* is a METAPHOR for rock-solid things that also don't require proof. • *I'm so grateful to have all of the people in my life still. It truly is a blessing and one that gets taken for granite.*

SIMPLYSHAYE.WORDPRESS.COM • 10 JUN 2014

granola oil

Confuses *granola* with *canola oil*, both of which are supposed to be good for you; the mistake is sometimes just the result of a missing comma between *granola* and *oil* in a recipe. • *In this recipe, I used olive oil instead of butter, you can use granola oil as well.*

WWW.BHOOKAJANTA.COM • 10 JUN 2014

grim and bear it

V: *grin and bare it*. Confuses *grimace* with *grin*. Often suggests someone *grimacing* and enduring an unpleasant situation. George Lichty's once-popular comic strip, *Grin and Bear It*, included a regular feature, "Grin's Fairy Tales," a PUN on the folklore work of the Brothers Grimm, which may contribute to the mistake. The variant is usually just a PUN. • *It's going to be gruelling, tough and very dark, but you don't need to grim and bear it on your own!*

WWW.NIGHTTERROR.CO.UK • 10 JUN 2014

gun-ho

Gung-ho was adopted as a slogan and battle cry by a battalion of US Marines in World War II; they understood it to be Chinese for *work together!* Ever since, it has connoted eagerness, often in association with *guns* and war. The EGGCORN might now be appropriate for gun enthusiasts advocating open-carry laws. • *We have been attending marriage counseling which he was gun-ho about until our therapist started telling him he was very wrong for certain things....*

gun-ho

WWW.FACEBOOK.COM • 11 JUN 2014

h

hack-kneed

A *hackney* was a riding horse, often an older one hired out or used to pull a *hackney cab. Hackneyed* came to mean old and overused. That might describe bad *knees*, too. • *Drew Brees will be the national perspective, likely with some hack-kneed reference to Auburn beating Alabama.*

WWW.CATSCRATCHREADER.COM • 11 JUN 2014

hailed into court

The antique legal term *haled before the court*, or *haled into court*, has mostly given way to the more COLLOQUIAL *hauled into court*. *Hale* (to drag forcibly) derives from Germanic words meaning *fetch*. However, *hail*, in the sense that taxis are hailed (called), is an EGGCORN. • *The rationale for this is that if the defendant has sufficient contact with the state, the defendant can reasonably anticipate the possibility of being hailed into court. . . .*

NATIONALPARALEGAL.EDU • 11 JUN 2014

hair-brained

hair-brained

Perhaps confuses *harebrained* with *airheaded*. *Harebrained* (rash, silly, or stupid) derives from the erratic mating dances of *hares*, as in *mad as a March hare*. It also follows that someone with *hair for brains* wouldn't be very sharp. • *A forthcoming paper proposes the latest hair-brained geoengineering scheme to allegedly offset global warming.*

HOCKEYSCHTICK.BLOGSPOT.COM • 11 JUN 2014

half-asked

Unconscious self-censoring at work: Rather than hearing the expression *half-assed* for what it is, the EGGCORN-ist assumes it must be something less vulgar and makes the substitution—which sort of makes sense in reference to an incomplete question. • *The thing is, Nintendo has never really given us a real multiplayer experience. They've always been half-asked.*

WWW.ZELDAINFORMER.COM • 11 JUN 2014

half-hazard

Haphazard means subject to *hap* (chance) and *hazard* (risk), as in *a roll of the dice* or *without any real plan*. The EGG-CORN version confuses it with phrases such as *half-assed* or *half-cocked*, conveying the same sense of unprepared-ness. • *Kentucky's taxing, spending and borrowing policies are half-hazard, at best.*

WWW.COURIER-JOURNAL.COM • 11 JUN 2014

half-mass, flying a flag at

Would flying a flag at *half-mass* be Flag Lite (all the flap-ping, half the mass)? Or something that happens *half-way* through a Roman Catholic Eucharist? Perhaps the EGGCORN connects the solemnity of the *Mass* to that of the flag tribute to recently deceased heroes. • *Is it not Half Mast when it is flying on a ship, half staff when it is flying on a flag pole? If so, when is it half mass?*

WWW.USA-FLAG-SITE.ORG • 11 JUN 2014

handfew

Confuses a *handful* and a *few*. It may result from writers who change their minds mid-sentence about which term to use. Yet the many examples to be found by Googling suggest it's often an EGGCORN for *handful*. • *Here's a hand few of the killer deals ripe for the picking in our Deals & Steals section.*

WWW.FACEBOOK.COM • 11 JUN 2014

hand-fisted

Rare. An adjective that confuses METAPHORS for *heavy-handedness*—*ham-handed* and *ham-fisted*—and the expression *hand over fist* by omitting the *ham* entirely. • *Everything we do is a hand-fisted clueless response to this baffling human condition.*

WWW.STANDARDCULTURE.COM • 12 JUN 2014

harbringer

V: *harmbringer.* Often just a misspelling. The ancient Germanic words *heri-* (*army*) and *-beorg* (*shelter*) are roots here; a *harbinger* was someone who scouted for an army, procuring or arranging food and shelter in advance for it. It has come to mean a signal that precedes something, which helps explain why it might also be perceived as *bringing* things. • *Do you believe democratic elections in Iraq were a harbinger of the Arab Spring of 2011?*

WWW.DEBATEPOLITICS.COM • 11 JUN 2014

hardy, party

V: *party hardily, wholehardily. Hearty* is often confused with *hardy* (but not the slight, dignified writer Thomas Hardy) and vice versa, depending upon whether one pronounces the *d* or the *t. Party hearty* (the original rhyming phrase) means *party strongly*; the EGGCORN *party hardy* might mean *party for a long time* or describe someone *able to endure many parties.* • *Party hardy with dance band Pardi Gras tonight at the Arboretum.*

POPCULTUREBLOG.DALLASNEWS.COM • 11 JUN 2014

hare's breadth

V: *a hair's breath, a hare's breath.* From *hairsbreadth*—the *breadth* (width) of a *hair* rather than the width of a *hare* (a wild rabbit that can be fairly thick if well fed). The dimensions of a hare's breath are hard to measure. • *NetScreen's price is double WatchGuard or SonicWall, but it ranks number two in total performance score, only a hare's breadth behind Cisco.*

hare's breadth

WWW.NETWORKWORLD.COM •

6 MAR 2014

hat at, try one's

Combines three IDIOMS: *try one's hand at, put on one's hat,* and *toss one's hat in the ring.* • *I really love the game, and missed it so I have come back now, to try my hat at it again.*

US.BATTLE.NET • 11 JUN 2014

heartship

V: *claim heartship, financial heartship.* Confuses *hard* and *heart,* perhaps influenced by *hard-hearted. Heartship* suggests that one has a good heart, no matter the circumstances to be overcome. • *Family Members taken on a non-command sponsored tour will be faced with financial heartship due to no logistical support.*

WWW.MILITARYINSTALLATIONS.DOD.MIL • 11 JUN 2014

heave scorn on

V: *heave contempt on.* Depending on how you like to deliver scorn, you could *heave* a heavy load of it at someone, or you could *heap* lots of smaller loads (the expected

IDIOM). • *Bill Clinton helped temper liberal ridicule of politicians with southern accents, but it's still fair game to heave scorn on rural otherness.*

WWW.POLITICO.COM • 26 SEPT 2014

hedgemoney

Hedge funds, which provide a *hedge* (protection) against losses in other investments, are *hedge money*. *Hegemony* means leadership and dominance, not money (although if you have enough hedge money it's easier to lead and dominate). • *Anything that threatens USA hedgemoney wether real or perceived is seen as a threat in the USA.*

WWW.POLITICS.IE • 11 JUN 2014

going to hell in a hen basket

hen basket, going to hell in a

Presumably a basket for collecting eggs from hens, and thus also an alternative to a *handbasket* as a proverbial route to damnation. The *OED* first records *going to hell in a handbasket* in the mid–nineteenth century, but that sort of playful alliteration is much older: Shakespeare's Hamlet boasts that when the wind is southerly he can tell a "hawk from a handsaw." • *Meanwhile, as the world goes hell in a hen basket, Antelope Valley is being dusted over.*

WWW.FACEBOOK.COM • 11 JUN 2014

here, here!

The British parliamentary cry *Hear! Hear!* supports a speaker's point, especially when the other side is trying to shout him down. The EGGCORN *Here! Here!* might convey the sense of *You've got support here!* or *I want it here!* • *I say here here to instant replay.*

WWW.ANSWEROLOGY.COM • 13 JUN 2014

here on end, from

A more definite version of *from here on in*, which has no *end* date. It may conflate the IDIOMS *from here on* and *in the end,* or *for weeks on end.* • *The company announced that the former $3.99 app would be free from here on end.*

STATESCHRONICLE.COM • 13 JUN 2014

heresy testimony

v: *tried for hearsay.* If you saw someone commit *heresy* (utter unorthodox religious beliefs) and testified to it in court, that would be "eyewitness testimony"; if someone told you that someone else committed heresy, and you testified to that, it would be *hearsay testimony* (or hearsay heresy testimony). You could be *tried for hearsay* if you published slander based on an overheard conversation. • *Judge Ott explained how the current law concerning heresy testimony relating to probation revocation in Georgia causes problems.*

WWW.INTERSTATECOMPACT.ORG • 13 JUN 2014

herlequin

Perhaps the female version of a *harlequin*, the jester-like character in pantomimes who wears a costume with a pattern of diamond shapes. It comes from *Herla*, a mythical king of faeries—*Herla cyning* in Old English. Usually just a misspelling, but an EGGCORN with regard to the intended audience for romance novels. • *There is a Herlequin Romance set in Victoria. One of the characters is a double-decker tour-bus driver.*

VIBRANTVICTORIA.CA • 13 JUN 2014

high bred

V: *hi-bred*. Historically, *hybrids* were anything but *high bred*. The word comes from the Latin *ibrida*, a word for the pigs of a domesticated sow and wild boar—and, by extension, "half-breed" children of parents of different races. • *I say fine, I get to try out that there Prius high bred car and see what its like.*

WWW.TRACTORBYNET.COM • 13 JUN 2014

higher, for

Hire is an old English word that has remained mostly unchanged for more than a thousand years, but it has nothing to do with *height*. Even so, employment does raise one's status and income. • *i know linux and java and pythhon and gml and batch and binary so please higher me also if u pay me i want 6/10 of the profits thx thx.*

WWW.MINECRAFTFORUM.NET • 13 JUN 2014

higherarchy

Hierarchy comes from the classical Greek for *sacred* and *ruler*, and traditionally the *hierarch* was holier, not stronger, than others. But we now tend to describe status and power in terms of *height*. • *The front label, which is on top in the higherarchy, is displayed on both the front and back of the bottle, and on the back it is backwards.*

BLENDERARTISTS.ORG • 13 JUN 2014

Hobbesian choice

Tobias Hobson, a British entrepreneur who rented hackney horses (see also HACK-KNEED), gave his customers *Hobson's choice* (i.e., no choice) about which horse they got. The philosopher Thomas Hobbes, remembered for the "Hobbesian" version of life in the state of nature as "solitary, poor, nasty, brutish, and short," tends to get credit for nasty, brutish choices. • *On the other hand, asking them to make a Hobbesian choice between two bitter outcomes this late in the game is a cop out by the countries leadership.*

THETREEOFLIBERTY.COM • 14 JUN 2014

hock (souvenirs, etc.)

V: *ad hock, hock a loogie. Hocking* (pawning) a watch means using it as collateral; *hawking* a watch means selling it. The two get mixed up, as do *hawking up phlegm, hacking* (coughing), and *hocking*; the last is just onomatopoeia, as few pawnshops offer much for phlegm. • *I own a printer. I should be able to do whatever I want with them, including printing out copies of the latest bestseller and hocking them on the street.*

BITCOINTALK.ORG • 14 JUN 2014

holidays sauce

V: *Holland Days Sauce.* The deliciously creamy French butter, egg, and lemon sauce known as *hollandaise* is suitable for *holidays*, especially when served with fish. Its name means *sauce of Holland*, so *Holland Day* isn't as wrongheaded as it seems. • *Photos of BabyStacks Cafe Hawaiian pulled pork with cabbage, eggs Benedict and holidays sauce on the side.*

WWW.YELP.COM • 15 JUN 2014

Holloween

Halloween gets its name from the holy—*All Hallows' Eve* (the evening before All Saints' Day), a former pagan holiday reframed by the Christian church as a time for praying for the souls of the dead. *Hollow* is a spooky-sounding word that can also mean *halloo* (hello) or *holler* (yell), but *Holloween* is usually just a misspelling. • *On the first day of Holloween The house gave to me. A vulture in a dead tree.*

WWW.AMIRIGHT.COM • 14 JUN 2014

hone in on

Confuses expressions such as *finely honed* (sharp) with *home in on* or *zero in on* (focus on, locate) and sometimes with *horn in on* (intrude upon). *Homing*, as pigeons perform it, often involves flying in narrowing circles until the target is reached. *Hone* means to sharpen; the MALAPROPISM conveys the sense of a carefully sharpened instrument and sometimes *cutting in*. Some dictionaries now accept *hone in on* as a STANDARD USAGE. • *Wow, lady, way to hone in on this kid's moment.*

TWITTER.COM • 17 SEPT 2014

host on his own petard

host on his own petard

V: *hosted by his own petard.* *Petards* are bombs, which few *hosts* find entertaining. Shakespeare's famous phrase *hoist with his own petard* describes someone hoisted into the air by the blast of his own bomb. Since the petard belongs to the person blown up, though, the connections with *host* and *hosted* have a faint logic to them. • *This protestor was literally host with his own petard.*

GLOBALECCO.ORG • 15 JUN 2014

human cry

V: *hew and cry.* The Old French word for a war whoop, *heu*, gives us *hue and cry*, a Norman legal term equivalent to an American sheriff's recruiting of a posse. It also describes a mob's demand for justice and thus could be seen as a *human cry. Hew* means a chopping blow to accompany the cry. • *Did any of you . . . raise the human cry, "Let's bomb them into the stone age?"*

WWW.WORLDSOCIALISM.ORG • 14 JUN 2014

hurdle

Hurtle comes from *hurt*, to move violently, smashing (hurting) everything in the way; it's an archaic word that got confused with *hurl* (to move as if thrown). *Hurdles* are temporary barriers, and jumping over them became known as *hurdling*. Hurdlers hurtle down a race track—some smashing through hurdles, some hurdling them. • *Kimbrell's experiments will center on fruit flies reared on the ground; fruit flies hatched on Earth and hurdled into space; and flies born reared in space.*

UCANR.EDU • 16 JUN 2014

hydroseal

Hydrocele is a medical term for fluid accumulated in a bodily cavity such as a testicle; -*cele* (from the Greek for tumor) gets confused with *seal* (from *sigil*, or *sign*), which means to close something, as wax seals a letter. • *Hydro Seal Operation—anyone else's little boy had it?*

WWW.NETMUMS.COM • 16 JUN 2014

i

illicit (sympathy, support, etc.)

Mix-up of a verb, *elicit* (to draw out), and an adjective, *illicit* (forbidden). These HOMOPHONES are often used in related contexts, as with attempts to elicit support for an illicit cause. • *Maybe some of them are trying to illicit sympathy from a co-believer.*

WWW.CITY-DATA.COM • 16 JUN 2014

immanent (peril, etc.)

Confuses the HOMOPHONES *immanence* (something that exists or dwells within, such as the spirit) and *imminence* (something about to happen). *Immanent* homicidal impulses in someone might represent a potential threat to others, but they'd become an *imminent* threat only when he picked up a pistol. • *Recently, whenever I meditate, I've been getting a sense of immanent danger. It's as if there's someone behind me, waiting to attack.*

WWW.MAGICKASCHOOL.COM • 19 JUN 2014

imperial evidence

v: *umpirical evidence.* Confuses *imperial* (of states ruled by an emperor) with *empirical* (of medical conclusions ruled by factual data) and sometimes with the rulings of a sports *umpire* (a neutral arbiter

imperial evidence

whose name comes from the French *nonper*, meaning *without peer*). *Imperial* units established by the British Empire included *inch*, *foot*, *yard*, *furlong*, *chain*, *league*, and *stone*. • *We don't have any imperial evidence or true data.*

CHARLOTTE.CBSLOCAL.COM • 2 JUN 2014

impremature on, put (your)

A conflation of *immature* and *premature*, confused with *imprimatur* and *imprint*. A hasty Roman Catholic writer might publish a childish tract prematurely, stating the church's views before imprimatur (official license and approval) is granted. *Impremature* also confuses *imprimatur* and *imprint* (a mark or impression) with, perhaps, *picture*. • *What he needs to do is to put his impremature on olmert or some other center right person.*

WWW.SILICONINVESTOR.COM • 16 JUN 2014

in able to

Confuses *enable to*, *in order to*, and *to be able to*, meaning the last. • *How much money do you need to earn a year in able to survive in the US if living alone?*

WIKI.ANSWERS.COM • 14 MAR 2014

in age, day

Confuses the clichés *in this day and age* and *in an age when. . . .* In this day and age it is common for writers to mix up the two. • *In this day in age, we are very busy individuals. We want to get information quickly.*

WWW.WEBRANGESOLUTIONS.CA • 22 MAY 2014

inclimate weather

inclimate weather

Clement comes from a word meaning calm, and *inclement weather* is not calm. *Climate* often describes the prevailing weather in parts of the world (e.g., Antarctica's climate is harsh, Hawaii's tropical). It derives from a Latin word having to do with the *inclination* of the sun at various latitudes. There's more to a bad climate than the latest bad weather. • *Recon Marines complete 237 mile "Hell Hike" in inclimate weather.*

WWW.OAFNATION.COM • 16 JUN 2014

incoming, up

Someone who's *up and coming* is on the rise, likely to make something of himself or herself. *Up incoming* suggests arrival in a surge. • *Sweden is an up incoming market, it has made great changes in its politics which will greatly benefit their market. . . .*

CAPS.FOOL.COM • 16 JUN 2014

incourageable

V: *encourageable. Incorrigibility* (inability to be reformed or corrected) has little in common with the inability to get courage—or the ability to be encouraged, for that matter. So this mistake appears to be a simple MALAPROPISM. • *You are afterall an incourageable attention seeker.*

WWW.THESCIENCEFORUM.COM • 19 JUN 2014

inherit goodness

V: *inheret goodness.* A thing that *inheres* is something essential that's internal, while those who *inherit* get something external from others. *Inherent* and *inherit* get confused because both words relate to qualities of ownership: You could inherit goodness inherent in your family. • *And each has the inherit qualities of true southern eating . . . Comfortable, handmade goodness.*

WWW.COLORFULPALATE.COM • 17 JUN 2014

in memorial

Confuses the related HOMOPHONES *immemorial* and *in memorium. Immemorial* means *old and unremembered*, while *in memorium* means something done *in memory of* an event or person so that it or he/she doesn't become immemorial. • *Since time in memorial, anchor texts have been very powerful SEO tools.*

WWW.CONSUMERHIGHFIVE.COM • 17 JUN 2014

in neck, neck

Artist H. R. Giger's famously creepy creature for the film *Alien* stretched out its neck and opened its jaws, and out came another neck and another set of biting jaws—a literal example of *neck in neck*. However, the phrase's use to convey the sense of *even* or *in close competition* is just a HOMOPHONE mistake for *neck and neck*, a racing term. • *They were neck in neck for 1st place for the 2nd classroom competition for the year.*

WWW.PINTEREST.COM • 8 JUL 2014

inpacked on

V: *inpacked wisdom tooth.* Confuses *impact on* with *impacted*. *Impact* describes one thing's collision with another; *impacted* is usually a dental term describing one tooth growing against another. In both cases, the EGGCORN ascribes an inward force to impact as well as impaction. • *I got my wisdom teeth pulled out here in VA when i first moved here. ALl 4 our my wisdom teeth were inpacked.*

WWW.MILITARYSOS.COM • 18 JUN 2014

part in parcel

in parcel, part

Part and parcel was a medieval real-estate term describing which land was included in certain deeds (the term *parcel* is still used today for that purpose). *Part in parcel* suggests something *included in* a package. Both the IDIOM and its EGGCORN convey the idea of inclusion. • *This is*

part-in-parcel to a major turnaround for airlines, in
general.

WWW.OUTSIDERCLUB.COM • 15 JUL 2014

intensive purposes, for all

Originally legal terminology, *for all intents and purposes* is now
just another commonplace such as *more or less* or *for the
most part* and means *pretty much*; the MALAPROPISM makes
the purposes more *intensive* but pretty much conveys the
same point. • *For all intensive purposes he is my muse.*

WWW.JAZZMINWINDEYPHOTOGRAPHY.COM • 18 JUN 2014

interfearence

Though some writers and protesters may *fear* that someone
will intrude upon them and *interfere* with their actions,
this word is usually just a typo-based error, not an EGG-
CORN. • *Does this mean that you dont want government
interfearence in your life or that you do?*

ABLE2KNOW.ORG • 18 JUN 2014

intergrade

Most segregated grade schools were *integrated* in the 1960s
and 1970s, which may help explain this EGGCORN. (The
perfectly correct biological term *intergrade* means an
intermediate form.) • *However, I would beg to differ that an
ending of prayer in schools and intergrading schools where
the cause of America's current ills.*

WWW.BLOGIT.COM • 18 JUN 2014

in-term

Confuses *interim* and *mid-term*. A temporary appointment
or a preliminary exam or report made in the middle of a
term might logically be referred to as *in-term*. However,

the conventional word is *interim* (from the Latin word meaning *between*). • *The Executive Board has the authority to fill a vacant position on the Board by an in term appointment.*

AAPT-NES.ORG • 18 JUN 2014

internally grateful

Aesop called gratitude "the sign of noble souls"; if so, it is an *inward* sign—something felt. You might indeed be *internally grateful*, but if you wish to convey the nobility of your soul to others, you tend to use spoken expressions of gratitude, such as the cliché *eternally grateful*. • *I'd like to add my list of six things for which I am internally grateful and I invite you to create you own list. . . ."*

WWW.THEFREEDOMZONE.COM • 18 JUN 2014

in the same, one

One and the same describes identicalness, as with two praying mantises that look the same. *One in the same* might describe one of the identical bugs eating the other. • *[A]rt is not separate from culture: they are one in the same.*

WWW.CULTURALSURVIVAL.ORG • 13 JUL 2014

intimate danger

intimate danger

Imminent means *about to happen*, and *intimate* means *close and personal.* Danger can be imminent without one sensing it, but generally a person in imminent danger feels it very intimately indeed. • *Unfortunately you are not in Intimate danger or life threatening, hes not inside your home. So call a cop.*

ANSWERS.YAHOO.COM • 18 JUN 2014

invincible hand, the

Sometimes a deliberate PUN about card games. Adam Smith's classic METAPHOR for the laws of supply and demand in a free-market economy, an *invisible hand*, holds that such forces are more or less *invincible*, and will self-correct if governments don't interfere. • *Where is the invincible hand of the marketplace headed?*

WWW.THEFREELIBRARY.COM • 27 JUN 2014

irregardless

Combines *irrespective of* and *regardless of. Irregardless* is a double negative, and hence should mean *with regard to*, not the intended *without regard to*. It suffers the stigma of double negatives (such as *hasn't got no sense*): No matter how often one cites the precedent of Chaucer, whose elegant Middle English poetry included many double negatives before the usage became unfashionable, it doesn't make no difference—people say it's a mistake. • *Irregardless of any proof, I will roll in Vegas with an open mind and an open notebook.*

WIZARDOFVEGAS.COM • 27 JUN 2014

isles, walked the

V: *walked down the isle.* Point-of-purchase *island displays* are freestanding shelves in prominent locations of retail stores; one could thus walk from one *isle* to another. Most writers mean *walking the aisles*, and the island METAPHOR breaks

walked the isles

down under close inspection: aisles surround freestanding shelves as water surrounds an island.
• *Way over priced and I walked the isles for 30 mins no one came to see if I need help.*

WWW.FACEBOOK.COM • 28 JUN 2014

j

jar-dropping

jar-dropping
Perhaps confuses *jarring* and *jaw-dropping*. Some accents are such that *jaw* is pronounced *jar*, which could also explain the mistake. Typically, however, this is an EGGCORN conveying the sense of someone *dropping a jar* in surprise. • *[Hall and Oates] was a jar-dropping show. Especially at that time when they were so hot.*

WBLM.COM • 29 JUN 2014

jewel, pus

A disgusting near-HOMOPHONE for *pustule* that imagines a *jewel*-like pearl of *pus* beneath the skin. • *Interesting, looks to me like a pus jewel from an ingrown hair or something that she got stuck in there.*

WWW.HORSEGROOMINGSUPPLIES.COM • 29 JUN 2014

jive with

You could indeed *jive with* someone if you were dancing, but the MALAPROPISM is used instead of *jibe with*, which means *to agree with something*. *Jibe* may come from the sailing maneuver where a boat's boom and sails shift from one side to the other when running

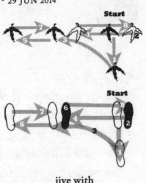

jive with

before the wind—presumably to a more *agreeable* point of sail. The *OED* suggests it might derive from *chime*, where bells ring in agreement and harmony. • *Teacher test reprieve doesn't jive with standards.*

WWW.ADIRONDACKDAILYENTERPRISE.COM • 26 SEPT 2014

juice-harp

V: *jaw harp*. The ancient metal device used to make mouth noises was first called a *Jew's trump* (trumpet), and later the more common *Jew's harp* (perhaps from its shape); the *OED* speculates that it was "made, sold, or sent to England by Jews, or supposed to be so." The name is now considered offensive, which may have led to the saliva-inspired EGGCORN. • *I'd really like to see someone put together some high quality sample sets of spoons a juice–harp and a washboard.*

WWW.KVRAUDIO.COM • 15 JUL 2014

k

key, on an even

Confuses the nautical METAPHOR *on an even keel* with the musical METAPHOR of harmonious *keys*; both suggest smoothness. Sailing ships with weight distributed *evenly* fore and aft tend to handle better. A minor key sounds discordant notes, so a more harmonious (or *even*) major key seems smoother. • *It made the process so much easier for me during such a stressful time, your sense of humor kept me on an even key when I felt like giving up.*

WWW.GREENVILLESCREALESTATE.NET • 5 AUG 2014

kill over

Keeling over employs the METAPHOR of a boat's capsizing to describe someone falling down—often fainting or dying, which explains the *kill* in the EGGCORN. It may also be informed by *overkill.* • *When we got around the corner I felt like I had run 5 miles and could kill over and die.*

WEARETHELAMARS.BLOGSPOT.COM • 29 JUN 2014

kit gloves

It's possible to imagine gloves kept in a *kit bag*, but what's meant is *kid gloves* (leather gloves made from the skins of young goats or sheep). They are thin and permit a delicate touch but are so rare these days that many writers using the cliché don't envision leather gloves at all. • *You get treated with kit gloves because everyone assumes you're gonna go berserk on them.*

JULIEMADBLOGGER.WORDPRESS.COM • 29 JUN 2014

knit-pick

V: *knitwit, pick knits.* Perhaps confuses picking *pills* of fabric from *knitted* cloth with picking louse eggs (*nits*) from hair. The EGGCORN doesn't convey the latter meaning's gaucheness: It's no compliment to refer to someone (or yourself) as a *nitpicker*, or public remover of lice. • *OH! and since everyone likes to knit pick at what a baby "shower" means, I have my own theory, Its called a "BABY" shower!!*

COMMUNITY.BABYCENTER.COM • 30 JUN 2014

knotical miles

Speed at sea is measured in *knots*, but a *nautical mile* per hour isn't a *knotical mile* per hour. Knots get their name not from the word *nautical* but from the knots on a measured rope called a *log line*, which is paid out behind a moving ship. A nautical mile equals 1.151 statute (land) miles, so 10 knots is faster than 10 miles per hour on land. • *We disembarked the ship after traveling 4080 knotical miles.*

WWW.TRAVELBLOG.ORG • 30 JUN 2014

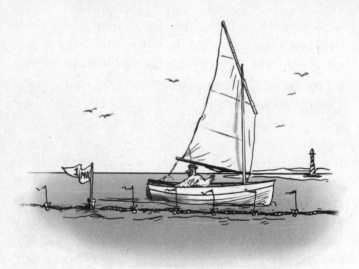

knotical miles

lagerheads, at

From *at loggerheads*, meaning at odds with; many arguments have broken out over beer, and *lager* forms a *head* of foam when poured. Interestingly, a loggerhead was a tool found in old-time taverns for making hot, foamy alcoholic beverages such as rum flips—a rod with a ball of metal at the end that was heated in a fire and plunged into the drink. The ETYMOLOGY of *at loggerheads* is unclear. It might come from whaling, where the *loghead*, or *loggerhead*, was a post built into a whaleboat's bow. A harpoon's hawser (rope) was given a round turn on the post during a battle between the whalers and the harpooned whale. Whalers and whale were thus *at loggerheads*. • *To a much greater extent the partizans have met at lagerheads with no evident winner.*

WWW.BETTORSWORLD.COM • 1 JUL 2014

lamb, on the

Lambs gambol, so you might imagine that running joyfully to escape capture could refer to them. But *on the lam* literally means *to beat it*—to run away. It derives from Germanic words meaning *to beat* or *to lame* a person or animal. • *This criminal who was on the lamb for a long time was identified by a cop who saw him walking across the street.*

on the lamb

WWW.ZDOUF.COM • 1 JUL 2014

lambash

A perfect EGGCORN, since the two words that compose it, *lam* and *bash*, basically mean the same thing as the real word, *lambaste*. *Lam* is an antique word meaning *beat*, and so is *baste* (to beat or thrash). *Lambash* just uses a more current word, *bash* (to hit or criticize). • *I wasn't enthused by his hire, but I never lambashed him either.*

WWW.TIGERSX.COM • 1 JUL 2014

lame man's terms, in

Suggests that if being a professional and an expert is cool, being an amateur and a *layman* is *lame*. • *For those of you who don't know, Ragnarok is today, or in lame man's terms, the Norse version of the end of the world!*

WWW.DEBATE.ORG • 1 JUL 2014

LAN line

Confuses a *LAN* (local area computer network) with a *landline.* Phone companies call the old-fashioned phone lines that run over copper wires and fiber optic cables *wireline systems.* Some customers, however, call such phones *landlines,* as opposed to *mobile (*or *cell) lines.* • *She doesn't have high speed internet, no cable, no cell phone (still uses a lan line) but she has a nice 1 bedroom apartment and a newish car. . . .*

WWW.MMO-CHAMPION.COM • 1 JUL 2014

lazy-fare

The English *lazy* (to dislike work) and the French *laissez-faire* (*leave it alone*) both suggest inaction. Yet laissez-faire economic policies would work hard at keeping business unimpeded, whereas lazy policies just wouldn't bother. The words have different origins, too: *Lazy* apparently derives from *lay* and *lie*, while *laissez* comes from *let* or *allow.* • *Study the Catholic answer to lazy faire capitalism called distributism and see how you can implement it in your own life.*

CHARLESCARROLLSOCIETY.COM • 1 JUL 2014

leadway

The nautical term *leeway,* used figuratively to mean *room to maneuver,* gets confused here with *lead time*, or *advance notice* for preparation. • *I assume that even for long trips they are not able to check bags so they must have some leadway to carry extras.*

WWW.FLYERTALK.COM • 2 JUL 2014

leaf on life, new

V: *new leash on life*. Combines *turn over a new leaf* and *get a new lease on life*. Both figures of speech have to do with paper—the first the pages of a book, the second a contract. The variant may confuse the *lease* IDIOM with *on a tight* (or *short*) *leash*, which, like a lease, is binding. • *But it could give the neocons a new leash on life, a way to invigorate their exhausted ideological engines.*

DISH.ANDREWSULLIVAN.COM • 17 SEPT 2014

leech field

Neither a *leech field* nor a *leach field* is a place you'd want to linger. The former would be marshy and full of bloodsucking worms

leech field

of the order *Hirudinea*; the latter would be sandy to filter septic system effluvia. *Leech* and *leach* can both be traced to ancient words for *lake*, and both extract things. • *My septic tank is old, cement but only one tank for solids and liquids. My leech field is not corrugated but the good old clay.*

WWW.PLUMBINGFORUMS.COM •

2 JUL 2014

social leopard

leopard, social

Parallels *social lion*, but marred by spots. The usual expression is *social leper*, which refers to the historical shunning of people with *leprosy*. The MALAPROPISM lacks the ugliness of the "correct" METAPHOR, which may encourage writers to make the mistake. • *She is treated like a social Leopard and leaves. Later Corny Collins see her dance and has her come on the show.*

ANGELABOUNDS.THOUGHTS.COM • 2 JUL 2014

liable suit

Libel comes from the Latin word for *book*, and libel was traditionally something untrue published in print. Now publication of libel in any mass medium is grounds for a *law*suit. Conviction in court can result in *liability* (from the Latin word for *binding*) for monetary damages and even criminal charges in some countries. • *Otherwise, the company opens itself up to a liable suit for opining what they "thought" of the individual.*

WWW.DSLREPORTS.COM • 2 JUL 2014

limp nodes

V: *limp edema*. The notion of *nodes* that are *limp* and that swell up has a certain logic to it. *Lymph* (from the Latin *lympha*, meaning *clear liquid*) circulates through the body and supplies white blood cells to fight infection; *lymphedema* is a condition in which nodes of tissue in the lymph system swell and retain fluid. • *My 5 year old has had swollen limp nodes in his neck.*

WWW.REMEDYSPOT.COM • 2 JUL 2014

links, car

V: *would go to any links.* Mistaken for *car lengths.* In stockcar racing, where racers are so close together that they seem *linked*, one might imagine a measurement based on *lengths* of *linked* cars. • *When you are on the road, you cannot predict what other drivers will do, which is why you should keep at least three car links behind the vehicle that is in front of you.*

BREAKUPNEWS.COM • 13 MAY 2014

lip-sing

Arguably all singing is *lip singing* (except perhaps Tuvan throat singing), but this confusion with *lip syncing* certainly seems logical. To *lip sync*, of course, actually means moving your lips and pretending to sing. • *This version has him looking even more awesome and has him awkwardly lip singing but it's ok.*

MOTORMOUTHSAYS.WORDPRESS.COM • 3 JUL 2014

load down, the

Confuses *the lowdown* with *download*, getting inside information as if you were downloading it from the Internet, and *on the down-low* (in secret). The late-nineteenth-century noun *lowdown* also conveys the sense of a *bottom line*. It comes from the adjective *low-down* (disreputable, such as a *low-down scoundrel*), which is much older. *The down-low* was African-American SLANG that often referred to homosexual activity. • *The twittersphere was buzzing with fans from all over the world staying awake to get the load down on the setlist for the tour.*

WWW.THECELEBCULTURE.COM • 3 JUL 2013

locust of, the

Locust and *locus* aren't related—the first comes from the Latin for *lobster*, the other from the Latin for *place*. Perhaps *locusts* suggests a cloud of insects whirling around a central *locus*. Writers might also see it as parallel to *focus* or *focused*. • *I teach a Modified Reading Recovery program so my professor told us to pick an action research project that was in the locust of our classroom.*

FORUMS.ATOZTEACHERSTUFF.COM • 3 JUL 2014

long behold

v: *low and behold*. The interjection *lo!* means *behold!* and vice versa; *lo and behold* just intensifies the interjection, and is used ironically by modern writers. *Long behold* makes some sense—essentially *take a good look!* But *low and behold* is just a misspelling, unless you're addressing cows. • *I checked my Experian report and long behold the Debt is no longer showing but no increase on the score?*

FICOFORUMS.MYFICO.COM • 3 JUL 2014

loss, no love

The *OED*'s first record of the cliché *no love lost* comes from the playwright Ben Jonson, in 1600. Here the expression undergoes REANALYSIS—as if the writer is reporting *no hair loss*—as a sort of status update. • *So you can see there is no love loss between the future Hall of Fame players that have been going at it for the last several years.*

SPORTS-KINGS.COM • 9 JUL 2014

lounge, chaise

A *long chair* (from the French *chaise longue*) has a long leg rest upon which you can stretch out—or *lounge*—and has given rise through FOLK ETYMOLOGY to *chaise lounge*. The mistake goes back to the early nineteenth century and now appears in many dictionaries as a STANDARD USAGE. • *When it's time to settle back and relax, try a Chaise Lounge, Leather Chaise Lounge, Reclining Chaise Lounge and more at Macy's.*

WWW.MACYS.COM • 14 MAY 2014

lover, land

Only a *landlubber* would say *land lover*. A *lubber* was originally a stupid lout, the word deriving from a French word for a crook. *Landlubber* was sailor SLANG for someone unused to the sea and its ways, though some landlubbers grow to *love* the sea. • *I must've looked like a real land-lover, walking around the deck, half crouched over like I had just soiled myself.*

WWW.SPORTINGLIFE360.COM • 3 JUL 2014

m

magnet, (cattle, land, shipping, etc.)

Many a *magnate* has a *magnetic* personality. *Magnet* derives from the ancient region of Magnesia, in

cattle magnet

Asia Minor (Turkey), source of magnetic lodestones. *Magnate* (an influential person) comes from the Latin word for *great*. • *Picture of Christina Onassis daughter of Greek shipping magnet Aristotle Onassis is seen at her flat at Avenue Foch in Paris France.*

WWW.WIREIMAGE.COM • 3 JUL 2014

might and mane

mane, might and **v:** *might and mien.* A lion exhibits *might and mane*, and a movie action hero may project a mighty *mien* (manner). However, the phrase *might and main* simply means *strength. Main* is an Old English word for strength that survives mostly in the alliterative IDIOM that pairs it with *might*—which also means strength. • *FirstGroup will be straining with might and mane, to win over as many new passengers as it can.*

WWW.BBC.COM • 3 JUL 2014

manner from heaven

Usually just a HOMOPHONE error. *Manna* is the mysterious substance that the Bible says sustained the Israelites in the wilderness, and the word comes from ancient Hebrew. *Manner*, which comes from a word related to *hand*, means the way things are done. One could say that the Israelites were fed in a miraculous manner, but it would just be a PUN. • *This Best Buy information is treated like manner from heaven for those of us bent on emulating scrooge!*

WWW.WHATPRICE.CO.UK • 4 JUL 2014

mano-on-mano

Mano-on-mano, or the correct Spanish IDIOM *mano-a-mano*, for that matter, has nothing to do with being a *man*—that would be *de hombre a hombre*. The EGGCORN confuses *man-to-man* (a basketball, football, or *fútbol* defensive tactic) with the Spanish expression for *hand-to-hand* fighting. A woman could settle things *mano-a-mano* just as easily. • *Mano on Mano: Who's the better player this season?*
WWW.ZIMBIO.COM • 4 JUL 2014

manor, bedside

Unlike *to the* MANOR BORN, this is more often a spelling error or a PUN than an EGGCORN—unless you learned empathetic behavior because you were born with a mansion next to your bed. • *Bedside manor I believe is part of a persons characteristic, but I believe can defiantly be taught.*

WWW.KEVINMD.COM • 3 MAY 2014

manor born, to the

The 1979–81 BBC situation comedy *To the Manor Born* punned on *to the manner born* (meaning *born with aristocratic ways*), a phrase coined by Shakespeare. But most people don't know that and use the EGGCORN version, which means *born in a manor* (a mansion) or *born rich*. • *She was to the manor born, a doctor, and "a glamorous figure who would always turn heads at political meetings."*

AUCONTRARIAN.BLOGSPOT.COM • 4 JUL 2014

marquis candidate

A *marquee* was originally a military field tent, later a canopy for a building entrance, and eventually a sign over a theatre that announced shows and actors. It came to mean *star*, like the actors it promoted. It has the same ETYMOL-OGY as *marquis*, a rank of nobility; in battle, some nobles stationed themselves at a marquee. • *Nor is he indebted to one marquis candidate who will expect him to direct all party resources to one high profile race.*

WWW.VOTECOREVALUES.COM • 5 JUL 2014

marshal law

V: *marital law.* A *marshal's law* and *martial law* aren't the same. The first is law enforced by a *US Marshal*. The second is law imposed by the military. A marshal was originally the official in charge of *mares*, or horses. *Martial* derives from *Mars*, the Roman god of war. *Marital* law derives from domestic battles. • *Marshal law has been declared by the military in Thailand following months of political unrest.*

WWW.MIRROR.CO.UK • 4 JUL 2014

marsh pit

marsh pit

V: *mush pit.* What began as a *slam pit* at punk concerts (an area in front of the stage where slam-dancers banged heads) was later called a *mash pit* and then a *mosh pit*—the name that stuck. It can indeed resemble a kind of swamp of sweaty, pogo-ing, slam-dancing bodies. The variant makes sense, too, as individuals may feel pounded to *mush* in the crush. • *Beyonce went nuts and even got in the marsh pit check out the photos when u read on.* . . .

martial your (strength, arguments, etc.)

Martial is an adjective, not a verb such as the standard *marshal*. Its associations with *marshal* and *muster*, both of which are military terms and can be used as verbs, make it a frequent EGGCORN. A field marshal (a general) could marshal his martial forces in March, and march all of them into a marsh. • *This action allows you to martial your resources to get things done while you're busy doing other things.*

mating name

Actually, a woman's *mating name* would be the name she took when she married, not the *maiden name* she had before she changed it. Unless, of course, she never changed it. • *Thats why mom still hasnt changed her mating name.*

meat, make ends

When one struggles to *make ends meet*, *meat* often isn't on the menu. But *making ends meat* isn't hard if you're a butcher cutting sirloin tips, chuck *ends*, and butt *ends*. • *If you're trying to make ends meat or otherwise can't be bothered with extra hassles, feel free not to worry much about this yet.*

medal, pedal to the

V: *pedal to the mettle*. The rhyming description of fast driving, *pedal to the metal*, is sometimes misspelled so that the rhyming words match. If you were cycling in the Olympics, you could in fact *pedal to the medal*. • *Putting the pedal to the medal should be done in nothing but style.*

INCH BY INCH, ROW BY ROW . . .

vegetable melody

melody, vegetable

Confuses *melody* with *medley*. The poet Andrew Marvell wrote to his coy mistress of his "vegetable love," so why not further delight her with a vegetable *melody* (from the Latin for *song*) such as a harmonious arrangement of peas and carrots? The usual word, *medley*, comes from the Latin for *mix*. • *Now you have a light and delicious vegetable melody. If you prefer a fruit salad you can use the same balsamic vinaigrette.*

metal, gold (silver, etc.)

V: *metalist, test your metal, gold (etc.) mettle. Medals* are usually made of *metal*, and the name may derive from that or from an ancient coin called a *mail*. *Metal* and *mettle* share an ETYMOLOGY, so you could also *test your mettle*, and see if it is as strong as steel, as thin as tin, or a noble *metal* like gold. • *In 2007, Kelly won gold and silver metals and in 2011 a bronze medal in the World Long Range Championships for individual and team events.*

mettle of honor

Those awarded the Congressional *Medal of Honor* have shown their *mettle* in combat. *Mettle* derives from *metal* and may actually have started out as a PUN or an EGGCORN. • *In fact, there is one dog that was awarded a mettle of honor I believe it was.*

IVF.CA • 5 JUL 2014

midland, fair to

The Scottish *middling* (of middle quality) was widely adopted by American cotton growers, for whom *fair to middling* became a standard grade and consequently a joking response to "How are you?" The MALAPROPISM might imprecisely associate *midland* with *average middle America.* • *Our meal and a tiny cup of chowder & one fair-to-midland drink was $45 each!*

WWW.TRIPADVISOR.COM • 4 JUN 2014

midrift

Confused with *midriff.* The ancient word *riff* (belly) only survives in *midriff.* Hitting a man in the *midrift*, perhaps in the sense of the *rift* (gap) beneath the ribs known as the solar plexus, might knock the wind out of him. • *It then hit him in the midrift and spilled out.*

WWW.WBAUNOFFICIAL.ORG.UK • 5 JUL 2014

mind-bottling

The adjective *mind-boggling* and the verb *boggle* probably come from old words for ghosts and spirits (such as a *bogey*). This linkage isn't intuitive when you want to describe *amazement.* The idea of capturing a mind in a *bottle* actually seems far more amazing. • *Where did my* half-brother come from? . . . *explores the mind of a young boy who [seeks to] . . . answer this mind-bottling problem.*

DRDIONNAHANCOCKJOHNSON.COM • 26 MAR 2014

mindgrain headache

A rare but vivid EGGCORN conveying the *migraine* sufferer's feeling that something is sending roots of shooting pain into his or her head. For those with visual symptoms, it can also convey the granularity or graininess of perception through the pain. • *I went down and told the front desk that I had a mind-grain/headache from the noise. . . .*

WWW.EXPEDIA.CO.TH • 7 JUL 2014

mist of, in the

V: *in the miss of.* Amid the well-known *fog of war*, you might choose to write of discovering hope *in the mist of* troubles. Sometimes this is just an issue of *mis*spelling *midst*, but some examples speak of clouds and shadows and are clearly meant figuratively. • *Well, this is a good segway to introduce my 5 practical points on ways to maintain peace in the mist of confusion.*

WWW.BREATHOFGODMAG.COM • 7 JUL 2014

mixmash

V: *mismash.* The EGGCORN and its variant are mashups of *mismatch, mishmash, mix-up,* and *mix 'n match* (or the British version, *mixy-matchy*). Interestingly, the EGGCORN appears only in the sense of mismatched socks, and not in the sense of a mismatch between David and Goliath. *Mishmash* (or *mish-mosh*) becomes *mismash* with the help of *mismatch* and *mashup.* • *This page still is looking like a mixmash between old & new styles to me.*

BUGZILLA.MOZILLA.ORG • 7 JUL 2014

mix words, not to

To *mince* means to chop into lots of little pieces; *mincing words* means using lots of words to hide your meaning. The expression most often appears in the negative *I won't mince words*. It's perhaps confused with getting *mixed messages* or sending *mixed signals*. • *Try not to mix words as it tends to confuse the stockability challenged. It also is not good to argue with an idiot. . . .*

INVESTORSHUB.ADVFN.COM • 7 JUL 2014

Monday (details, concerns, etc.)

Mondays are *mundane*, and this confusion is a natural one. *Mundane* means *of the world* or *dull*; the beginning of the workweek, with its pursuit of worldly necessities, certainly qualifies. • *Luckily, we're here like a little ray of sunshine in your drab Monday existence . . . with another awesome episode.*

WWW.THEFREEFINANCIALADVISOR.COM • 8 JUL 2014

morning dove

Zenaida macroura, the *mourning dove*, gets its name from what the Cornell Lab of Ornithology describes as its "soft, drawn-out calls [that] sound like laments." The bird's call is familiar to people on early *morning* walks or runs, which may account for the EGGCORN. • *During my walk to the summit, I saw only one bird. A lone morning dove perched upon a wire.*

WWW.THEWESTENDNEWS.COM • 8 JUL 2014

motherload

Gold mining isn't part of the public imagination much any-more. That's why the METAPHOR of a *mother lode*—a large deposit of gold with many "daughter" seams extending from it—seems a less likely source of rewards than a *mother* and the *load* of things she provides. • *Yes, all of my non-blogging is leading up to the mother load of all tag sales . . . and it's THIS WEEKEND!*

FWTX.COM • 8 JUL 2014

mustard, pass

Combines the IDIOMS *cut the mustard* and *pass muster*, both of which convey the idea of qualifying. The *OED* identifies *cut the mustard* (or "cut it") as SLANG for having what it takes to succeed, and *pass muster* as a military METAPHOR for sur-viving inspection. Or it could mean sharing condiments.

pass mustard

• *When you pass mustard and are BST forum eligible, you may post a want ad there, should get you plenty of hits.*

WWW.STRIPERSONLINE.COM • 15 JUL 2014

mute point

V: *mood point*. *Moot* comes from the same Germanic word as *meet*; a *moot point* describes an irresolvable dispute for which further meetings are fruitless. As there's no point in talking about it, it's a *mute point,* too—or even a *mood point,* if the lack of resolution depresses you. • *I know this is a mute point, but why are the stupid MSM not calling New Mexico and Iowa (Vanity).*

WWW.FREEREPUBLIC.COM • 8 JUL 2014

my as well

Confuses an optional personal action with *might as well* and *may as well. Might* and *may* both talk about a future or conditional action, and tense confusion ensues. • *Cant find anything by this band on here so I my as well post some stuff.*

WWW.GUITARETAB.COM • 8 JUL 2014

nail, death

Dead as a doornail is a cliché that gets mixed up here with the ringing of bells, or *death knell,* that marks a funeral. Another confusion might be with *coffin nails.* Interestingly, one maker of crossbow arrows markets its bolts as "death nails." • *Krayton Kerns is angry because he believes that birth control is the "death nail in the coffin of our Republic."*

MTCOWGIRL.COM • 22 MAY 2014

narrow, straight as a

Usually a typo for *straight as an arrow* rather than an EGGCORN; a Google search produces no examples of archers with only one *narrow* left in a quiver. However, some writers might have a different METAPHOR in mind: The terms *straits* and *narrows* describe similar geographic features, and the King James Bible's way to salvation is *strait* and *narrow* • *I had been making a conscious effort that week more than normal to fly straight as a narrow and to be the righteousness of God.*

WWW.REVEAL.ORG • 8 JUL 2014

naval gazing

naval gazing

Usually a PUN. You might say that the difference between an *omphaloskeptic* and a *skeptic* is that the first *gazes at his navel* whereas the second gazes askance. This MALAPROPISM confuses *omphaloscopy* with watching ships. Both can be leisure activities, but the *navel-gazer* is more self-absorbed. • *Although some scholars have criticized various forms of reflexive ethnography as self-indulgent naval gazing, I believe it is naval gazing with a sociological eye.*

BOOKS.GOOGLE.COM • 8 JUL 2014

never regions

May confuse *nether regions* with *Neverland* from *Peter Pan* or the *Never-Never Country* of Australia's outback. Nether regions get their name from an old Germanic word for *below*, traditionally Hell or the Underworld. • *Toilet humour, eye-watering blows to the never-regions and*

Evel Knievel–style stunts are on the Jackass (3D) *menu in this film.*

FILMGAZE.COM • 8 JUL 2014

next-store neighbor

This would be a perfect EGGCORN if its writers referred only to neighboring merchants. However, many examples refer to *next-store neighbors* in residential areas. Linguist Mark

next-store neighbor

Liberman characterizes it as "phonetically similar if not identical to 'next door,'" so it seems to be a case of sound overriding sense. • *My next store neighbor, who doesn't know I have this page, just complimented me on my abs.*

WWW.FACEBOOK.COM • 8 JUL 2014

nipples in a twist, don't get (your)

British English refers to twisted underpants as *knickers in a twist.* There are many American English examples of *don't get your underwear in a twist* or *don't get your panties in a bunch,* but the British version is heard here as something more painful sounding. • *Just don't expect me to get my nipples in a twist over your caterwauling about some architecture.*

WWW.FREEREPUBLIC.COM • 9 JUL 2014

not, all for

V: *all for knot, come to knot.* Confuses *it was all for naught* with *it was not to be.* The variants suggest the idea of a knotty ending. • *I have pleaded with everyone for help and it was all for not.*

www.tv.com • 9 JUL 2014

nozzle of a gun

nozzle of a gun

A gun has a *muzzle*, and a hose has a *nozzle*. This EGGCORN appears to confuse a *snub-nosed pistol* with a gun muzzle or with the idea that a gun can *spray* bullets. • *Since the recent [incident] five and a half thousand of our fellow citizens died from the nozzle of a gun.*

www.cityweekly.net • 9 JUL 2014

nugget, chewy

Nugget originally was a Scottish term for a short, compact person or animal, and later an American term for a small, compact chunk of gold. *Nougat* comes from the Latin word for *nut* and describes a chewy mix of nut and candy. • *Milk chocolate with a soft chewy nugget top and crunchy cereal bottom.*

choco-locate.com • 15 MAY 2014

O

oaks, feeling your

V: *sow (your) wild oaks.* An uncommon mistake. The expression *feeling (your) oats* comes from horses' getting frisky after feeding, but the EGGCORN (or acorn, in the case of the variant) appears to refer to the strength of a mighty *oak* tree. • *Me thinks that you are still "feeling your oaks" and when you mature a little more you will see the need to make the correct choices.*

feeling your oaks

ANSWERS.YAHOO.COM • 9 JUL 2014

of forethought, malice

V: *malice and forethought.* The legal term *malice aforethought* is used to distinguish manslaughter (which isn't planned, or *aforethought*) from murder (which is). So the EGGCORN *malice of forethought* (evil forethoughts) is not incorrect English, but it's not a legal term, either. • *Kelly Wayne King, 54, was arrested in early June and charged with first-degree murder—malice of forethought for the death of Terry Stuart, 62.*

WWW.SEQUOYAHCOUNTYTIMES.COM • 3 JUL 2014

off-quoted

v: *off-repeated, off-times.* Many public officials claim they have been *off-quoted* (misquoted), but the MALAPROP-ISM usually just confuses the antique and poetic *oft* (often) with the more familiar *off*, perhaps in the sense of *told off* or *knockoff.* Ofttimes it even sounds correct. • *He also referred to the off quoted analogy of a claim to a fenced field.*

WWW.JURISDICTION.COM • 10 JUL 2014

Old-Timer's disease

Usually a PUN or grim joke, though there seem to be a few genuine examples of children and others getting it wrong when referring to *Alzheimer's disease.* • *I'm working every day. I don't want to end up with old-timer's disease.*

HAMPTONROADS.COM • 10 JUL 2014

olé, café

The Spanish shout *¡olé!* comes from *¡hola!* (*hey! hi!*) and means *bravo!* But it's clearly an exotic word to English speakers, which explains why it gets confused with its HOMO-PHONE, the also-exotic French coffee-and-milk beverage *café au lait.* • *On* [Sex and the City], *Carrie just ordered a cafe ole. I've been googling it for 10 minutes and still can't find out what it is.*

FORUMS.VOGUE.COM.AU • 12 MAY 2014

once so ever

Whatsoever is an old word that combines two other old words—*whatso* (whatever) and *soever* (whenever)—to create an intensifier, *nothing ever.* You could simply say "He found nothing," but "He found nothing whatsoever" is stronger. The EGGCORN *once so ever* drops the *whatever* part and makes the intensifier focus more on the element of time. • *Please unban me, I have done nothing once so ever to any of you or your server, ever!*

CIAGAMING.ORG • 10 JUL 2014

on mass

En masse (in a group), *en bloc* (all together), *en banc* (an entire judicial bench), and similar French phrases are rich sources of MALAPROPISMS. Some linguists argue that they aren't malapropisms at all but examples of a foreign language absorbed into English and given a meaning similar, but not identical, to the original. • *A few employees and I were not happy with the bonus that we were offered and all resigned on mass.*

WWW.I-RESIGN.COM • 14 JUL 2014

on quote, quote

V: *quote endquote.* In dictation to a stenographer, quotations were begun by the speaker saying *quote* and terminated by the speaker saying *unquote*, which became a convention in radio and TV journalism. *Quote on quote* suggests a series of overlapping quotations; *quote endquote* is an example of hypercorrection. Typographers may distinguish between quotation marks as "open quotes" and "close quotes." • *Hell, I think that describes 95% of the people who start a quote-on-quote 'diet.'*

WWW.TONYGENTILCORE.COM • 14 JUL 2014

on route to

V: *in route to.* Linguist Arnold Zwicky argues that *on route to* is an example of English speakers "nativizing" the

French *en route*, which has occurred for so long that it shouldn't be considered a MALAPROPISM at all—except by those with a fetish for French pronunciation. However, most dictionaries include entries for *en route* but not *on route* or *in route*, so it's not fully assimilated yet. • *This time tomorrow we will be flying on route to the Gold Coast. #yay.*

TWITTER.COM • 18 JUN 2014

on timely (death, demise, etc.)

Someone late for his or her own funeral might avoid an *on-timely death*, but this MALAPROPISM probably doesn't make sense, since the meaning of *untimely death* is "early or unexpected death." • *The Oscar was received by Michelle Williams on behalf of Heath Ledger due to his on timely death.*

WWW.PINTEREST.COM • 14 JUL 2014

on-tray

on-tray

A main course (*entrée*) some-times arrives on a tray rather than just plated, so this mis-take makes EGGCORN-ish sense. • *It's a very delicious meal that many enjoy but restaurants might just be going over top withe this delicious on tray.*

MES15S.EDUBLOGS.ORG • 14 JUL 2014

open mined

V: *open mine. Open-pit mines*, often known as quarries, are ecologically destructive eyesores. Boosters of their eco-nomic benefits might ask you to keep an *open mind* about them. You might also imagine memories as something to be *mined*, or a *mine* as a METAPHOR for memory. • *Wes looked at Mark, "As a man of science, I must keep an open mined on all things."*

WWW.FANFICTION.NET • 14 JUL 2014

option, money is no

For the rich, money may be *no object*, but for the poor, it's *no option*. Actually, the original expression means that money literally isn't an object—a "thing" that's an obstacle. The EGGCORN version suggests that it's not an important choice you have to take into consideration. • *What is the best blue tooth ear piece out there? Money is no option (getting paid by the company. Woo hoo).*

WWW.SHARKYFORUMS.COM • 14 JUL 2014

our fours

Confuses *getting down on our knees* with *getting down on all fours*. It's not a mere HOMOPHONE mistake, though, as no one seems to write *our fours* in the first person. Instead they write *my fours*. • *Had we walked on our fours and resembled a bitter gourd, we'd pass off as crocks.*

NEURORHYTHM.WORDPRESS.COM • 7 JUN 2014

outer body experience

Perhaps confuses paranormal, psychic, or near-death *out-of-body experiences* with extraterrestrial encounters such as alien abductions—especially by aliens from Pluto, Uranus, Neptune, or other *outer bodies* in our solar system. • *Has anyone had an outer body experience or has died on the table and came back to life?*

US.TOLUNA.COM • 14 JUL 2014

out on a limp

May confuse the exposure of *going out on a limb* with the image of someone *limping out* into battle. It makes sense as an EGGCORN in that going out on a limb means taking a chance and leaving yourself vulnerable, as would going into battle while wounded. • *I'm going out on a limp and say "yes", and it's not because of Google's dominance in most other digital categories.*

BLOG.SYSOMOS.COM • 14 JUL 2014

own (your) success to

V: *own to, owning to*. The difference between *owing* and *owning* is the difference between getting a mortgage loan to pay for your house and paying cash for it. The result may sound similar, but there's an important distinction. One could take *ownership of his success*, or *own up to his success*, but that would be different from being indebted to someone else for it. • *I own my success to my parents, my wife, to this community, to my church, and to the grace of God.*

ALTHOUSE.BLOGSPOT.COM • 14 JUL 2014

p

packed, have it down

In early English, *pat* meant a blow that knocked someone *down*. By Shakespeare's time, *down pat* had come to mean information that one knew perfectly (and could recite). *Down packed* suggests that you *pack* the needed information into your head (perhaps employing a blow to make it fit). • *Then High School came and I finally had it down packed, I officially wanted to become some type of nurse.*

ADMISSIONHOOK.COM • 30 MAY 2014

pack with the devil, make a

Presumably you could *pack* your HEN BASKET before going to hell. If not, this EGGCORN suggests that a *pact* (agreement) *with the devil* might be like a *pack* that burdens you—or else hiring really incompetent movers. • *This is what happens when you make a pack with the devil, "Why Wall St. Is Deserting Obama."*

WWW.DEMOCRATICUNDERGROUND.COM • 14 JUL 2014

pail, beyond the

V: *over the pail*. The Pale in medieval Ireland was territory controlled by the English; those from *beyond the Pale* were considered wild, uncouth, and socially unacceptable. STANDARD USAGE now tends to include the sense

beyond the pail

of *crossing the line*. Poured water that misses its target, splashing *beyond the pail*, is also unacceptable and messy—and an EGGCORN. • *If physically touching hands (either by shaking or high fives) is still beyond the pail, then try using the thumbs up at each other. . . .*

WWW.FRESHEXPRESSIONS.ORG.UK • 6 MAY 2014

pain staking

Connoting affliction (being *staked out* to die, perhaps), this EGGCORN for *painstaking* is oblivious to the notion of *pains* as hard, detail-oriented efforts. • *If you have a lake house, you know what pain staking work it is to keep your beach and water front area looking beautiful.*

JEFFWEND.HUBPAGES.COM • 15 JUL 2014

palindrone

Palindromes (from the Greek word for *running back again*), which read the same way in both directions, can be long and monotonous rather than clever, *droning* on in the way of "A man, a plan, a cat, a ham, a yak, a yam, a hat, a canal—Panama!" • *What is the longest palindrone?*

WWW.CHACHA.COM • 7 APRIL 2014

pallor over, cast a

Confuses a *pall* with a *pallor*. A *pall* is a cloth (traditionally purple) that covers a corpse and gets its name from the Latin *pallium* (*cloak*); it also means haze that dims the sun. Bad news might *cast a pall* over events. *Pallor* is paleness, especially of facial features. • *That has cast a pallor over consumer spending, which accounts for more than two-thirds of the nation's gross domestic product.*

ABCNEWS.GO.COM • 15 JUL 2014

pansy-waist

V: *pansy-waste, pantywaste, pantyweight. Pantywaists* were one-piece children's garments consisting of panties and a top together; they came to connote *crybabys*. *Pansy* is a derogatory term for an effeminate man, so the combination doubles down on the insult. A *pantyweight* might be a puny boxer, smaller than a flyweight; *-waste* suggests *good-for-nothing*. • *Pay no attention to the wussie pansy waist know nothing Hollywood critics who diss this film.*

BLOG.CHRON.COM • 15 JUL 2014

paper-view

This MALAPROPISM for *pay-per-view* would be an EGGCORN only if cable TV subscriptions permitted you to view the book instead of watching the movie (though perhaps Amazon.com is working on that). • *I watched it on paper view it was FABULASS, it was great to see some one just come out swinging.*

WWW.D-SERIES.ORG • 15 JUL 2014

parrot-phrase

A bad *paraphrase*, perhaps? Usually a PUN. To *parrot* is to imitate slavishly; to *paraphrase* is to convey something's meaning with different words. • *So, let me parrot phrase this back to you, because I think I've found a gem here.*

parrot-phrase

FORUMS.HAPPYLATTE.COM •

15 JUL 2014

partition, sign a

Diplomats François Georges-Picot and Sir Mark Sykes signed a 1916 agreement that led to the *partition* of the

Ottoman Empire's Middle Eastern realms. The pact
carved them up to create Iraq, Syria, Jordan, Palestine,
Saudi Arabia, and a lot of future ethnic and religious
strife. *Petitions* of protest or advocacy are typically less
consequential. One could, of course, sign a partition petition. • *Get students to sign a partition, send the complaint
to the department of education and get her fired!*

POLYRATINGS.COM • 15 JUL 2014

path the way

v: *pathe the way.* The noun *path* comes from old Germanic
words for a footway, while the verb *pave* comes from a
Latin word for *flattening.* The similarity of the *v* and *th*
sounds helps explain the confusion. • *This will be very effective in helping me prepare for the future because it paths
the way to success.*

JENNAMCHENRY.WEEBLY.COM • 15 JUL 2014

peace about, said (my)

Conflates *said my piece about* and *made my peace with.* To *say*
or *speak one's piece* is to make a short prepared speech or
to voice an opinion. To *make one's peace* with something
is to be reconciled to it, which sometimes requires speak-
ing one's piece. • *I already said my peace about the FCC
new rules on the internet itself, but I would like to know
what you guys think.*

PLUS.GOOGLE.COM • 16 JUL 2014

Peace Core

A military *corps* gets its name from the Latin for *body,* from
a body of soldiers, while the origins of *core* (meaning *center*) are uncertain—perhaps from *corps,* perhaps from *cor*

(Latin for *heart*). Those who miss the oxymoron of the name *Peace Corps* might reasonably assume it means *peace center*. • *How can i join the peace core or something similar so i can travel for free to Korea?*

peak, a fit of

V: *peak your interest*. A *piquant* taste is sharp, and *a fit of pique* (irritation) is sharp, too—the word comes from the French for *prick*, or *irritate*. A *peak* has a pointed summit, and a peak experience is a high point—so the confusion with sharp emotions is understandable. When you're the most irritated, one could say you've reached peak pique. • *In a fit of peak the other day I did uninstall Chrome and as a result lost all my damn bookmarks. . . .*

pedal stool, on a

A *pedal stool* helps short-legged kids use piano pedals, but neither it nor the guitar-like instrument called a *pedal steel* resembles a *pedestal*. That comes from the French term meaning *foot of the seat*, describing the base of a column, which might resemble a stool to some. • *I can remember a time in my life where I put this man on a pedal stool and probably thought he was God.*

pension for, has a

Penchant and *pension* come from French words meaning *to incline* and *to pay,* respectively. Someone with a *penchant* (an inclination) for whittling might like carving wooden soldiers, for example. Waiting until you've retired with a *pension* (a regular retirement payment) to try things for which you have a *penchant* might qualify as an EGG-CORN. • *My current project is with a client who has a pension for shabby chic mixed with baroque glam!*

WWW.JESSICAHASTEN.COM • 16 JUL 2014

pepperika

Paprika is Hungarian for a sweet, peppery spice, a diminutive of *pepper* (to the effect of "li'l pepper"). Linguists have traced the word *pepper* back to before the ancient Greeks, well before the invention of goulash. • *Add pepperika, salt and oregano. . . . Pour the white sauce over the pasta and cook for five minutes in the pan.*

WWW.TASTEOFBIHAR.COM • 16 JUL 2014

peon to

Paean was one of the names for the Greek god Apollo, and songs of praise to him are *paeans*. A *peon* (which comes from the same Latin word as *pawn*) was a lowly footsoldier. In our unheroic modern world, poets write paeans to peons rather than gods. • *He would become increasingly more reactionary following the First World War and ultimately wrote a peon to the fascists in 1941. . . .*

BOOKS.GOOGLE.COM • 16 JUL 2014

perils of wisdom

Alexander Pope observed that "a little knowledge is a dangerous thing," so by extension, wisdom might well be *perilous. Pearl of wisdom* goes back at least to the 1700s; earlier English writers sometimes spelled *pearls* as "perils," but the word's origin has nothing to do with *peril* (danger). Pearls are, however, associated with the perils of diving. • *His perils of wisdom have yet to leave me, and I doubt they ever will.*

CA.RATEMYTEACHERS.COM • 16 JUL 2014

per say

The Latin *per se* can mean *in itself*, *as such*, or *without reference to anything else*. The EGGCORN confuses it with phrases such as *you might say* or *one might say*, which are used as similar interjections. Interestingly, the *ampersand* (&) gets its name from the phrase *and per se*—an example of the EGGCORN process at work. • *Joyce Flax said she isn't per say against another Walmart store in Sioux Falls.*

WWW.KDLT.COM • 17 JUL 2014

perspective (students, etc.)

Art students often study *perspective* (creating the illusion of three dimensions in two-dimensional art), but *prospective students* (those who are *prospects*) applying to college actually tend to lack perspective. That's why college visits are so important. • *Each meeting and perspective student visit are worth one credit.*

WWW.ARTSCI.UC.EDU • 17 JUL 2014

photogenic memory

If you had a *photogenic memory*, would you remember only those who looked attractive? This probably qualifies as an EGGCORN: The suffix *-genic* describes something that is well suited to doing something—in this case, looking good in pictures—and a *photographic memory* is often able to recall things as if they were pictures. • *These successful presentations of support for a photogenic memory have been documented on normal people with even more success.*

WWW.DEBATE.ORG • 2 MAY 2014

physical year

v: *physical hardship*, *physical deficit*, etc. Confuses *fiscal year* with *calendar year*, perhaps influenced by memories of the name of the celebrated *International Geophysical Year* of 1957–1958, which encouraged international scientific cooperation during the Cold War. *Fiscal* and *physical* are near-HOMOPHONES, and both are adjectives that are often mixed up in bureaucratic jargon. • *Budget for physical year 2011–2012 has been developed and will be discussed at August meeting.*

WWW.LOUISIANAKC.ORG • 17 JUL 2014

pier-to-pier network

May confuse a computer system with the communication between fishing sites at the beach. A *pier* extends out from land into the water or supports a span of a bridge. *Peer-to-peer networking* means there is no central hub that links a network of processors that share a computing load. It's often used by file-sharing services to evade copyright law and sometimes as a place for phishing. • *We are a pier-to-pier network and store our databases on a shared Network Access Device.*

WWW.TUTCITY.COM • 18 JUL 2014

pigeon English

Pidgen originally was a mispronunciation of *business* in China; it now means informal cross-cultural languages

comprising simplified vocabu-
laries. It's a HOMOPHONE for
pigeon, and the well-known use
of the birds to carry messages
may add to the confusion. • *We
spoke pigeon English and French
but I learned that the man was a
doctor who looks after "non-
citizens" in Nantes.*

Aloha, Cuz. Where you pau hana?

pigeon english

THIRSTYCYCLIST.COM • 18 JUL 2014

pigment of your imagination

Usually a PUN. Confuses *pigment*, in the sense of a colorful
imaginative vision, with *figment*, a word deriving from
the Latin *figmentum* (*formation, image*), from which we
get the word *fiction*. • *Maybe what my daughter saw was a
pigment of her imagination or is there really a Pinoy squirrel?*

WWW.PINAYMOMBLOGS.COM • 18 JUL 2014

pincher movement

V: *pinscher movement*. A *pincher* is someone who pinches; a
pincer is a tool for pinching. The military tactic known
as a *pincer movement* seeks to pinch an opposing army
between two attacking forces. The variant suggests an
attack by a pack of Dobermans. • *This operation of going
from Marburg to Paderborn was a planned pincher movement of enclosing an army of 376,000 German soldiers.*

WWW.3AD.COM • 18 JUL 2014

pipe, come down the

V: *come down the shoot*. Turnpike roads, or *pikes*, historically
exacted tolls from teamsters and cattlemen driving their

herds to market, or *coming down the pike* (arriving). This EGGCORN seems to confuse that expression with one derived from logging flumes, which would shoot tree trunks *down the chute* to a river or railroad. • *With all the beautiful images that come down the pipe from Hubble, our Solar System has been left with celestial body image questions. . . .*

PHYS.ORG • 18 JUL 2014

Pipe Piper

"The *Pied Piper* of Hamelin" is an ancient tale made popular by the Brothers Grimm. Yet few who hear of it these days know that *pied* describes the colors of the piper's dappled clothes. So the *Pipe Piper* might be understood as someone who pipes on his pipe. • *And they rode off down the Vegas strip with a bunch of Irish for a day drunks following close behind like the pipe piper.*

WWW.LEFTCRANIUM.COM • 18 JUL 2014

pit in (your) stomach

The cliché *a feeling in the pit of (your) stomach* describes the hollow feeling produced by anxiety, which is not the same thing that one feels after eating the pit of a peach or cherry. The *OED* lists *pit of the stomach* as another name for the epigastric fossa. • *When I saw the welcome email, I had a pit in my stomach. "So, I'm really doing this I guess. . . ."*

SARAHFIT.COM • 14 AUG 2014

pits and pieces

Dribs and drabs, bits and bytes—why not *pits and pieces* as an alliterative pair? It may be a typo by writers who start out to write *pieces*, then change their minds to say *bits and pieces*. • *Read some of her poetry, check out some pits and pieces of her upcoming story, and even get a few peaks at some of her art work.*

GENTLEANDQUIET.COM • 18 JUL 2014

plain geometry

A *plain* is flat, as is a *plane*, but there's also the notion that the introductory geometry taught in high schools is "plain" (ordinary), while the more complex, non-Euclidean geometries studied by math majors are harder and fancier. • *When I studied plain geometry, I learned and memorized the so-called Pythagorean Theorem.*

WWW.CPRF.CO.UK • 18 JUL 2014

planter warts

v: *planter fasciitis*. The word *plantar* (sole) shares the same origins as the word *plant*. *Plantar warts* are small, crusty growths on the soles of the foot caused by the human papillomavirus; *plantar fasciitis*, or jogger's heel, affects tendons in the heel and foot. Neither condition is limited to *planters*. • *On the other hand, unlike other warts, the planters warts on feet can be quite painful and often cause trouble walking.*

GETTINGRIDOFWARTS.HUBPAGES.COM • 21 JUL 2014

plays the piper

Confuses the legend of the *Pied Piper* of Hamelin with the saying "He who *pays the piper* calls the tune," meaning that the one who hires the band determines what gets played. • *Al Jazeera plays the piper, but Qatar calls the tune.*

PEACENEWS.ORG • 21 JUL 2014

playwrite

A maker of plays was a *play-wright* (play-builder), which
stems from the tradition of putting on a show in which
plays evolved as they were performed. The modern notion of an author's sitting down to *write* a play from
beginning to end, as a novel is written, influences this
EGGCORN. • *Additionally, he is a playwrite and lyricist, creating original scores for many children's productions.*

WWW.DOWNTOWNPAC.COM • 21 JUL 2014

pneumatic device

pneumatic device

When the Michelin Man has to
remember something, he may
employ a *pneumatic device*. For the
rest of us, a pneumatic device
would be something like an air-
powered lug wrench. A *mnemonic
device*, from the Greek *mnēmōn*
(*mindful*) rather than from *pneuma*
(*wind*), helps one remember
things. • *Earth's atmosphere (you
know, Troposphere, Stratosphere, etc.) Does anyone have a
pneumatic device that could help me remember this?*

ANSWERS.YAHOO.COM • 21 JUL 2014

point of you

Confuses *your point* with *point of view*. It could be an EGG-
CORN if the first person is referred to as the "I" *point of
view* and the second person is the *point of you*. • *That
point of you is, sorry, complete NONSENSE!*

WWW.THEZOMBIEINFECTION.COM • 21 JUL 2014

poke-a-dot

How dots became associated with the *polka* craze in Europe isn't known. *Poke-a-dot* has a logic that seems reasonable, though—a pattern of dots that resemble holes poked in a cloth. • *She'll stand out in this Toddler Girl's Poke-a-Dot Tunic from Carter.*

poke-a-dot

WWW.SHOPYOURWAY.COM • 21 JUL 2014

posed to (do something)

The verb *poised* means balanced, as when a cat is *poised* to jump. One could *pose* as if *poised*, and it would appear much the same. Some writers, reproducing DIALECT, use *'posed to* instead of *supposed to*. • *I agree with all of the above, they took the words right out of my fingertips when I was posed to begin typing a comment.*

JPGMAG.COM • 21 JUL 2014

postdramatic stress disorder

Trauma can be *dramatic*, so its confusion with the medical condition *post-traumatic stress disorder* has logic to it. A stage actor repeatedly confronted after the show for bad performances might experience *postdramatic stress disorder*. • *A lot of the time the problem with soldiers experiencing Post Dramatic Stress Disorder is that they are left living.*

AMS1BS12.WORDPRESS.COM • 21 JUL 2014

postpardon depression

Some ex-convicts granted *pardons* describe experiencing depression after leaving prison. It's odd, however, to confuse it with new mothers whose severe *postpartum depression* can lead to suicidal or homicidal thoughts. • *Have they tested your thyroid levels for post pardon depression?*

WWW.DRUGS.COM • 21 JUL 2014

pour over

The verb *to pore* (to read or study closely) is antique, used today only in conjunction with *over* or *through*; it may derive from the same origins as *peer*. The EGGCORN *pour over* conveys the sense of pouring one's attention upon something being studied. • *My children dropped what they were doing and ran to the living room floor to pour over the book.*

RUNNINGWITHTEAMHOGAN.COM • 21 JUL 2014

poweress

If you exhibit *prowess*, you show your knightly expertise and skill—the word derives from a French word for *valor*, so the confusion with *power* is understandable. • *And Ben, I'm most relieved you don't plan to discuss your sexual poweress on my blog. I'm quite sure we could all do without that.*

WWW.STUFF.CO.NZ • 22 JUL 2014

powerhorse

Confuses *horsepower* and *powerhouse*. The inventor of steam engines calculated one horsepower as what it takes for a horse to pull 150 pounds from a 220-foot-deep hole in a minute. Modern scientists have estimated that a strong horse (a powerhorse?) can actually generate more than

19 horsepower in short bursts.

powerhorse

• *Diego Rubio (Efapel) has proved to be a real powerhorse during the first two stages of this Vuelta a Castilla y León.*

WWW.CYCLINGNEWS.COM • 22 JUL 2014

preannual

Perennial comes from the Latin for *each year* and is often used to describe *evergreen* plants that bloom every year. This EGGCORN confuses it with *annual* plants, which bloom only one time. Perhaps a *preannual* is one that grew last year but not this year. • *Can anyone identify this preannual shrub that grows spines at least 10 ft each year?*

WWW.FLOWERSFORUMS.COM • 22 JUL 2014

preemptory challenge

Legal procedure allows lawyers to disqualify potential jurors without explanation, a tactic known as a *peremptory challenge.* It's easily confused with *preemption*—acting first by doing (or buying) something before anyone else gets the chance. The adjective *peremptory* comes from similar roots, but describes an order that says, in effect, "Just do what I say and don't argue!" • *I already decided to exercise a preemptory challenge to strike juror No. 7. I had the sense that she was biased.*

WWW.VALOREMLAW.COM • 22 JUL 2014

pre-fixed menu

V: *pre-fixe menu.* The French dining convention of a fixed-price (or *prix fixe*) menu is the opposite of an *à la carte* menu, from which you choose whatever items you want and add the prices of each. But it is chosen for you before it's cooked (or "fixed"). • *We ordered from the pre-fixed menu and were delighted with our choices.*

WWW.OPENTABLE.COM • 22 JUL 2014

pre-Madonna

V: *prime madonna.* Before there was *Madonna*, there were Lulu, Odetta, Melanie, Cher, and a number of other female singers known only by their first names. Many of these *pre-Madonnas* were doubtless *prima donnas* or, as we'd now call them, divas. • *On the flip side, he can also lose games for his side with a fiery temper that gets his team mates backs up—a true pre Madonna!*

WWW.CLUBWEBSITE.CO.UK • 22 JUL 2014

president, set a

The US Supreme Court's *Bush v. Gore* case *set a President* in office but argued that it should not be seen as *setting a precedent* (establishing a rule based on what was done before). Usually just a simple MALAPROPISM. • *When the U.S ended woman suffrage it set a president for other countries.*

PREZI.COM • 22 JUL 2014

preying mantis

Praying mantises are known as fierce hunters that *prey* on other insects (and on one another), so this is an easy mistake to make. The insect's name comes from the posture of its bladelike forelegs, which resemble arms in *prayer*. • *It's not exactly being there at three in the morning when the colt is born all legs and looking like a preying mantis.*

ESPN.GO.COM • 22 JUL 2014

professioncy

Confuses *professional* and *proficient*. *Professions* traditionally required schools or authorities to profess publicly that one was qualified. *Proficiency*, which usually requires practical skills rather than a degree, comes from a Latin verb meaning *to make*. • *[I] would be particular about his or her professioncy in handling at least one of these softwares.*

WASIMISMAIL.COM • 22 JUL 2014

q

quaffed

One might *quaff* the "hair of the dog" to cure a hangover, but hair is usually *coiffed*, not consumed as a beverage. • *My hair was quaffed a la Tony Curtis. My next suit was my best ever.*

ALFRESCO43.COM • 22 JUL 2014

quaffed

quick claim deed

The legal document known as a *quitclaim deed* is used to transfer property but lacks certain guarantees. It is often used between family members because it is *quicker* and doesn't require title research. That's why *quickclaim* would seem to qualify as an EGGCORN. • *Can you get a quick claim deed done in one state if the property is in another state?*

BESTANSWER.CO • 22 JUL 2014

radify (the agreement, etc.)

Usually just a typo or misspelling of *ratify* (sign or agree to) rather than an EGGCORN. May be influenced by *rad* or *radical*, both of which are used COLLOQUIALLY to indicate the approval of an idea. • *Both sides have to radify the agreement through voting, but that shouldn't take too long.*

HOCKEYLEAKS.COM • 23 JUL 2014

range to, give free

V: *free rein chicken, give free reign to.* Confuses *free range,* animal husbandry that allows chickens and other farm animals to graze or forage free of cages, with *free rein,* allowing horses to run without reining them in and a METAPHOR for independence. • *After honing his skills in several famous restaurants, where he nourished his culinary creativity, he decided to give free range to his own style.*

WWW.CHATEAUXHOTELS.CO.UK • 8 JUN 2014

rain of terror

V: *rain supreme.* The HOMOPHONES *rein, rain,* and *reign* get mixed up in a number of MALAPROPISMS and EGGCORNS. This confuses the *rain of fire* on Sodom and Gomor-

rain of terror

rah (Genesis 19:24) with France's *Reign of Terror* (1793–4), when it must have seemed as if terror rained down like brimstone. • *Are you accusing Nelson M of a rain of terror? He had to do what he had to do.*

WWW.BBC.CO.UK • 22 JUL 2014

raise a raucous

V: *make a raucous.* Confuses the nouns *racket* and *ruckus* with the adjective *raucous. Ruckus* means a riot or revolt, while *raucous* describes a tone—loud and harsh. So a raucous ruckus would raise quite a racket. • *Human ashes raise a raucous at Four Corners National Monument.*

WWW.DAILY-TIMES.COM • 22 JUL 2014

ranking file

A *ranking file* might be a *file* folder that contains the *rankings* of draft prospects or job candidates. It's more likely to be a MALAPROPISM for *rank and file*—the METAPHOR of "ordinary soldiers" marching in a parade. *Rank and file* often describes ordinary members of Congress, while *ranking member* is a title given to certain congressional leaders. • *Both parties will need to talk to the ranking-file members.*

WWW.U.TV • 22 JUL 2014

rapid, running

V: *running rabid.* Medieval heraldic devices (such as coats of arms or banners) often featured wild animals *rampant* (crawling or rearing), whose fierceness was meant to overawe foes. *Running rampant* came to be a synonym for *running wild.* It's a short step from *rampant* to the EGG-CORN *rapid*, which suggests *moving quickly*—or *rabid*, for that matter. • *But a stomach virus was running rapid in my home and that night it was my turn.*

WWW.MDJUNCTION.COM • 22 JUL 2014

rapid fan

rapid fan

Fan is short for *fanatic*, so a *rabid fan* would describe a fanatic crazed as if infected by rabies. A *rapid fan*, on the other hand, would be a fast-moving fanatic—a MALA-PROPISM but not an EGGCORN. • *In 1967, Star Trek came into the World and created a rapid fan base.*

WWW.LUKEW.COM • 22 JUL 2014

rather, something or

Conflates *something or other* (meaning *something*) with *or rather (to be more precise),* likely because of the near-HOMOPHONE pronunciation of *or other* ("or ruther") and *or rather.* • *But I gave it up within a week when I read a verse in the Bible that said something or rather about it being wrong to refuse to eat meat. . . .*

NOURISHINGMYLIFE.WORDPRESS.COM • 27 JUL 2014

ravished (with hunger)

Confuses *ravenous* (hungry as a raven) and *famished* (extremely hungry) with *ravished* (abducted and raped) and *ravaged* (devastated). May also be influenced by the adjective *ravishing,* often applied to objects of beauty, which had the original sense of something so sexually enticing as to inspire rape, but which now simply means *attractive.* • *The alert in the Tate gallery restaurant came just as I was raising my first forkful, ravished with hunger.*

WWW.TELEGRAPH.CO.UK • 21 SEPT 2014

rebel-rouser

V: *rubble-rouser.* Sometimes all it takes for a *rabble* (a disorderly crowd) to become *rebels* is a *rousing* orator to awaken passions. If the speaker is standing on the *rubble* of bombed-out buildings, it's even more dramatic. • *So, Barabbas was a rebel rouser. He was viewed the same way as many people saw Jesus.*

WWW.SERMONCENTRAL.COM • 23 JUL 2014

reconnaissance, released on (your) own

Another example in which the modern MALAPROPISM would once have been considered correct. *Recognizance* (a legal promise or bond) derives from the Old French *reconnaissance* (recognition), and someone *released on (his) own recognizance* simply *recognizes* his obligation to appear in court when called. • *I was released on my own reconnaissance and was scheduled to appear in court a month later.*

BRITISHEXPATS.COM • 23 JUL 2014

reels its ugly head

The cliché *rears* (or *shows*) *its ugly head* was common as far

back as the mid–1700s, and no one knows its source for certain. The MALAPROPISM would appear to have come from someone angling for large catfish. • *The conservative double standard reels its ugly head, yet again.*

reels its ugly head

WWW.CITY-DATA.COM • 23 JUL 2014

regiment, exercise

Military rules require soldiers to work out regularly, so *exercise regiment* has a certain logic to it. *Exercise regime* and *exercise regimen*—both meaning an exercise routine—actually derive from the same root as *regiment*: the Latin word for *rule*. • *What is your exercise regiment like?*

WWW.MYFITNESSPAL.COM • 23 JUL 2014

reign in

V: *don't rein in my parade, right as reign, reigns of power*. The HOMOPHONES *rein*, *rain*, and *reign* result in many MALA-PROPISMS. It makes some sense, for example, that laws that derive from a king's *right* as a *reigning* monarch are *right as rain*, or that you wouldn't want the excitement of a parade *reined in*, as a horse is reined in, any more than you would want it to *rain on your parade*. • *However, With-*

*erspoon reigned him in with more body work. The attack
withered Beale's spirit and had him breathing heavily.*

WWW.PHILLYBOXINGHISTORY.COM • 23 JUL 2014

rest bite, welcome

A *rest bite* might be a brief taste of rest. *Respite* derives from
the Latin for *refuge*, or *consideration*, and a *welcome respite*
is a period of relief. • *In a world dominated by electronic
dance music, proper indie guitar bands are a welcome rest-
bite from relentless auto tuned beats.*

THEWAVEUCA.WORDPRESS.COM • 24 JUL 2014

ride, laugh

Perhaps conflates expressions such as *a wild ride* or references
to roller coasters with *a laugh riot*. A *riot* can mean a public disturbance or a multicolor display. • *He also joked,
"Issue 11 deals with foreign aid to countries in Africa—so
it's a real laugh ride."*

WWW.NEWSARAMA.COM • 24 JUL 2014

right of passage

Confuses *right of way* with *rite of passage*. The former is the
legal right to use a particular route, the latter a ritual of
initiation (such as a bar mitzvah) that admits one to certain privileges. • *We trust this right of passage will leave
them each feeling more confident, empowered and prepared
for the next stage of their life.*

WILDEARTH.ORG • 24 JUL 2014

rights, last

Perhaps confuses the liturgical *last rites* read to a dying person with the Miranda *rights* read to a person who has
been arrested. • *As the priest read him his last rights in the*

hospital, he decided to chase a new distinctive sound integrating industrial and dubstep.

TWITTER.COM • 24 JUL 2014

rimming with

V: *rimming over.* An EGGCORN for *brimming with*, perhaps influenced by an advertising slogan for Brim coffee ("fill it to the rim with Brim") or by the sports description of a missed basketball shot or golf putt that "rims out." The *brim* was traditionally the edge of the sea, and *to brim* was to overflow. • *Eyes rimming with tears, she added, "Hopefully, I'll be like that when I'm that age."*

WWW.NYTIMES.COM • 24 JUL 2014

ring (his) neck

V: *ring (her) hands.* May confuse the traditional way of killing a game bird or chicken—by *wringing its neck*—with a *ring-necked pheasant* (*Phasianus colchicus*). *Wring* (to squeeze) has a slightly different origin than *ring*, though both are old Germanic words. Someone who *wrings her hands* might make a *ring* of one hand and squeeze the other. • *Wow i'm furious I want to ring his neck literally.*

WWW.FACEBOOK.COM • 24 JUL 2014

ringbear

A *ring bearer* at a wedding is traditionally a little boy who carries the groom's ring, and it's not hard to imagine one being referred to as EGGCORN-ishly as a kind of cuddly *teddy bear.* Since *bear* is a term of affection used by gay men, a *ringbear* might be found at a gay wedding as well. • *All three children that will be the ringbear and flow-*

ergirls are so precious, I will love love photos of them like this.

ringbear

WWW.PINTEREST.COM •

23 JUL 2014

ripe with (corruption, etc.)

This EGGCORN makes sense: The word *corruption* literally means *rot*, so something *ripe with corruption* would actually be overripe, or *rotten*; *ripe* can also describe a stink. *Rife* (which shares word origins with *river*) actually means widespread, generous, and overflowing. • *The story shows how these lease-leaseback schemes are ripe with corruption.*

EMERYVILLETATTLER.BLOGSPOT.COM • 24 JUL 2014

road to hoe, a tough

Early *roads* were indeed built with *hoes*, rakes, and shovels, and they were *tough* to build, but they aren't the source of the METAPHOR for a daunting task. The rhyming phrase *a tough row to hoe* comes from farming and refers to crops overgrown with weeds. • *That would be a tough road to hoe, but you can certainly have a local lawyer investigate.*

WWW.AVVO.COM • 4 AUG 2014

roast, chickens come home to

Confuses *roasted chicken* with *roosting chickens*. Often a PUN but sometimes a simple MALAPROPISM, probably a result

chickens come home to roast

of a misspelling or typo. Chaucer wrote that curses are like "a bird that returns again to his own nest," and the saying means that your evil deeds will come back to trouble you—not to embarass you in front of friends. • *However, Iran has done everything possible to avoid blowback or the chickens coming home to roast in its own territory.*

IGNORINGOCCUPATION.BLOGSPOT.COM • 24 JUL 2014

rod iron fence

V: *rot iron fence.* Sometimes a straightforward EGGCORN, in that *wrought-iron fences* are made of ornately hammered *iron rods*; and sometimes not, in that some iron fences are made of simple (rather than blacksmith-wrought) *iron rods* and are advertised as *iron rod fences* or *rod iron fences.* The variant lacks the logic of a true EGGCORN, since iron rusts but doesn't *rot.* • *An ornate rod iron fence surrounds a pebble bottom pool and spa.*

WWW.GOOGLE.COM • 24 JUL 2014

role call

May confuse a *roll call* with a *casting call.* In school it might qualify as an EGGCORN in the sense that a teacher takes the attendance of those in the *role* of "student." • *Now it*

was time for the role call
by states. It was a very
emotional time.

role call

root to

V: *route cause.* Confuses the METAPHORS of a *root* (source) with a *route* (path to) and may depend on whether one thinks the final product grows naturally or must be arrived at. • *Is it money or software thats the root to success[?]*

roughshot, running

V: *ride roughshot.* Perhaps confused with *grapeshot* or other kinds of *cannon-* or *gunshot.* Usually when horseshoes are nailed to a horse's hooves, the ends of the nails are nipped off by the farrier. But cavalry warhorses often went *rough-shod* (with the nails protruding) for better traction and to better trample enemy soldiers. • *Marion's own Zach Randolph has been running roughshot through the league of late.*

route, learn by

Confuses *rote* and *routine*, two words that aren't related. *Rote* is a Middle English word for *custom*, whereas *routine* derives from the French *route*, or *road*. Someone's routine was their regular route, but they often had to learn multiplication by repetition, or rote. • *Einstein did not learn by route memorization of facts, and reliance upon authority.*

RATIONALWIKI.ORG • 25 JUL 2014

rye expression

A *rye expression* might be something such as "I adore pumpernickel"—which might prompt *wry expressions* on the faces of those who do not. *Rye* is an ancient word for grain that hasn't changed much for thousands of years. *Wry* (meaning *twisted*, as with an expression that might be twisted with disgust), is almost as old. • *With a rye expression, Earle told reporters, "Our job is to prosecute abuses of power and to bring those abuses to the public."*

WWW.FREEREPUBLIC.COM • 25 JUL 2014

S

sacreligious

Sacrilege originally meant *stealing sacred things*, whereas *religious* (describing monks and nuns) meant *bonded by vows*. Someone whose actions are *sacreligious* may thus have nothing to do with their *religiousness*—although the logic of the EGGCORN is obvious. • *[Sampson] is chained in the temple by the Philistines and forced to witness a sacreligious act.*

WWW.PATHEOS.COM • 25 JUL 2014

sail (them) down the river

In antebellum America, *selling* enslaved people *down the*

river usually meant putting them on a riverboat to cities such as Memphis and New Orleans, which had active slave markets. Some of the riverboats were indeed sail-powered. • *There was a term for it back in the day, Sail them down the river.*

WWW.FACEBOOK.COM • 25 JUL 2014

sand hill, what in the

Rare. *The Sandhills* is a region in the Carolinas; *sandhill* may also refer to any sand dune. Numerous theories explain what the old American expression *what in the Sam Hill?* refers to; the most convincing is that it's simply a euphemism for *hell.* • *What in the sand hill are you trying to say here?*

TOWNHALL.COM • 25 JUL 2014

sandscript

A MALAPROPISM derived from the image of ancient writing found on sandy rock. *Sanskrit* actually comes from ancient India, where it is a language, and means *perfected*—the perfected language with which the great Indic myths are told. • *What do people think of the oldest known written religion written in sand-script, the Upanishads?*

UK.ANSWERS.YAHOO.COM • 25 JUL 2014

savor, time

The Latin saying *carpe diem* (*seize the day*) could be paraphrased as *savor your time on earth*, which may explain this EGGCORN. It confuses *savor* with *saver*, though of course a *time saver* allows one to savor more of the remaining time. • *I'm not sure why it took me this long to figure out*

*how to make it like this, but it sure is a time savor with a
hungry toddler at your feet!*

CHOCOLATEANDCARROTS.COM • 4 AUG 2014

scolding hot

scolding hot

A *scold* was originally a
skald—the word derives from
the old Scandinavian term
for a satirizing poet. But *scald-
ing* comes from the Latin *cal-
idus* (hot), although some
satirists can certainly deliver a
hot scolding. • *Discover all the
tastiest scolding hot coffee recipes,
hand-picked by home chefs and other food lovers like you.*

WWW.PINTEREST.COM • 25 JUL 2014

scrapegrace

A *scapegrace* is a mischievous person who escapes divine
grace, so perhaps a *scrapegrace* does a little better and
scrapes by. • *So I guess the Idea I'm getting at is that Bee-
thoven was a scrapegrace.*

HANNAHCARMODY.WEBS.COM • 3 JUN 2014

segway

The Italian word *segue* first described a smooth musical tran-
sition, as in "the *segue* between the *diminuendo* and the
crescendo," and came to describe smooth transitions in
general. The EGGCORN suggests transitions as a *way* between *segments*; its use preceded that of the *Segway* brand
for two-wheel electric vehicles and may have influenced

the name. • *Also to be cast, will be a male a female narrator to segway between topics.*

TURTLEONE.COM • 25 JUL 2014

seize and desist

V: *seize fire, never seizes to amaze. Cease and desist* orders are legal threats, and *seizure* of property is an enforcement tool of the courts. Sometimes they are used in concert. • *I have tried faxing them a sieze and desist order and they have lied to me and gave me the wrong number.*

UNKNOWNCALLERDISCUSS.COM • 25 JUL 2014

self-depreciating

Deprecating originally had to do with praying against, and to *deprecate* someone was to designate them as evil. *Self-depreciating* came to mean being modest about oneself. To *depreciate* someone is to disparage them; *self-depreciating* means disparaging oneself, which is different from *self-deprecating* modesty. • *Carrie took center stage interacting with the audience, self-depreciating herself and making it awfully hard not to like her.*

WWW.CHICAGONOW.COM • 26 JUL 2014

self-phone

V: *cellfie.* One could argue that a *cell phone*, which you carry around with you, is a kind of *self-phone*. Since most people take *selfies* (self-portraits) with their cell phone, *cellfie* is perfectly logical, too. • *I would give you my self-phone number but I am not sure if you are some kind of a cyberstocker or not?*

NIKOLHASLER.COM • 25 JUL 2014

sense worth, (my) two

The British expression "(my) two pennies' worth" may have come from the Gospel story of the "widow's mite" (the poor woman who gives some of the few pennies she has). It became (*my*) *two cents' worth* in America. Its irony (the suggestion that it's not worth much) qualifies a statement of opinion, and it gets confused with phrases such as *(my) sense is*, or *(my) sense of it is*. The EGGCORN is less ironic: Two out of five senses is certainly a much higher proportion than two out of a hundred cents. • *I normally dont get on topix and run my mouth . . . but when i saw this post i had to put my two sense worth in.*

WWW.TOPIX.COM • 27 JUL 2014

set and done, when all is

V: *after all is set and done.* The cliché *when all is said and done* dates from Elizabethan times and means *in the long run.* It distinguishes between words and actions, unlike the EGGCORN, which basically just offers two words—*set* and *done*—that convey the same sense of things that are finished. • *So when all is set and done I have jogged/walked 4 miles.*

IHOWTOGETASIXPACK.COM • 27 JUL 2014

severely, jointly and

Confuses *severally* (distinctly) and *severely* (strictly, seriously), meanings that are sufficiently different to prevent this from rising to the level of an EGGCORN. *Jointly and severally* is often used in legal documents to mean *as a group and individually*; *jointly and severely* would mean *harshly on the group.* • *8 years ago I was convicted of a crime and ordered to pay 34000 "jointly and severely" between 6 other people.*

sew, rip what you

V: *reap what you sew.* Often a PUN. Saint Paul's famous agricultural METAPHOR (Galatians 6:7) that *whatsoever a man soweth, that shall he also reap* had nothing to say about embroidery even though he was a tent mender by trade. The variant is generally just a

rip what you sew

HOMOPHONE error and not an EGGCORN. • *While I do believe in the security of the believer, I also believe you will rip what you sew.*

shape out

Confuses *shape up* with *shake out*, and perhaps with the commonplace phrase taken from the title of H. G. Wells's speculative novel *The Shape of Things to Come*. The idea that the future's *shape* will show itself is certainly EGGCORN-y. • *I do have a plan going forward, but I will admit that I do not know how things will totally shape out.*

sheik (fashion, etc.)

Since the twentieth-century oil boom in the Middle East, the image of the Arab *sheik* has evolved from that of a feudal desert warlord to that of a wealthy, sophisticated, international businessman—a possessor of *chic* luxury goods, which may help explain this mistake. • *He was supposed to be some uber sheik fashion designer hired to make the hot pockets?*

WWW.TIVOCOMMUNITY.COM • 28 JUL 2014

shift, short

Medieval criminals were given a *short* time before execution in which to confess their sins to a priest and be *shriven* (forgiven). *Short shrift* has come to mean something that gets not much time or attention, such as the work that can be done during a *short shift* at work. • *I was given short shift by the rude officer who quipped "would you rather have a criminal in your neighborhood or a helicopter."*

WWW.FACEBOOK.COM • 29 JUL 2014

shoe-in

shoe-in

A *shoo-in* is a sure winner in a horserace—perhaps one that has been rigged so that the rider need only *shoo* the horse across the finish line. Usually just a HOMO-PHONE error, but possibly confused with a *horseshoe* (connoting luck) or *soft-shoe* (dancing). • *If you look only at his time with the Braves, from 1996 to 2007, you would think he would be a shoe-in.*

WWW.KMALAND.COM • 28 JUL 2014

shore supply, in

v: *shore term*. May be confused with *inshore* (near shore).

The adjective *short* goes back to Middle English; *short supply* was sometimes used with regard to shipments arriving in port (on *shore*) short (lacking a portion) of what was expected. *Shore term* may bring to mind a sailor's short liberty call in port. • *However, the Consortium also recognizes that spending constraints are such that government capital available for such projects is in shore supply. . . .*

WWW.DRIFTPILECREENATION.COM • 29 JUL 2014

short-sided

Shortsighted describes nearsightedness—the inability to see or venture far ahead. The EGGCORN may refer to a team that is one or more members *short* of a full complement and thus is not able to proceed effectively. • *IMO its a little short sided of him to do away with the idea so quickly.*

WWW.HPIBAJAFORUM.COM • 29 JUL 2014

shutter to think

The cinematic image of *shutters* banging and rattling on a spooky old house may inform this confusion with *shudder*. The cliché *shudder to think* dates from at least the early 1700s. • *I shutter to think what Trenton's expressive language would be like if I didn't start getting him the help he needed two years ago.*

TWOBROTHERSONEJOURNEY.BLOGSPOT.COM • 29 JUL 2014

sick my dog on (you)

V: *sic my dog on (you)*. Not a MALAPROPISM at all—though many imagine that it is. *Sic* is more common in America (preferred by the *American Heritage Dictionary*) while the British *OED* prefers *sick*. It derives from an attack or chase command given to dogs in years gone by: *Seek!* or

Seek 'em! Neither has anything to do with the Latin *sic* (thus) that some readers may suppose, or with *sickness*, as some speakers assume. • *"So that shows you I am better than you and don't disagree or I will sick my dog on you."*

signal out

Perhaps confuses *single out* with *call out*, with *signal* used in the sense of a gesture. Spell-check and autocorrect programs may contribute to the mistake, since a search of old titles in Google's book database reveals only a few pre-computer-era examples of *signal out*. • *So, why was I signaled out for punishment? Why? Because I'm fat white conservative bastard that's why!*

I dub thee Sir Loin.

sirname

sirname

V: *sir loin*. Some Icelandic last names are literally *sirnames* (or *patronymics*, based on the father's name), such as Ericsson, if Eric is the father. In English, *surname* actually means a name added on (from the French *sur*, meaning *on top of*) to a person's first (or Christian) name. The variant was originally *surloine*, but it was EGGCORN-ized into meat fit for a noble or a knight (a "sir"). • *It seems they assumed his sirname was that of my family.*

siteseeing

A straightforward EGGCORN—*sightseeing* generally involves *sites*. The word *site* has nothing to do with *sight*, however, and derives from the Latin for *place*. • *We were early so went siteseeing until about 5 PM. We were able to park on the strret just around the corner and bring is our luggage.*

WWW.EXPEDIA.COM • 29 JUL 2014

skewered view, a

Confuses *skewer* (to spear something) and *skew* (to change position). *Skewer* is a METAPHOR for successful satire or criticism, particularly of someone with whose opinions you disagree. One might skewer a skewed point of *view*. • *Your opinion shows a skewered view from a selfish perspective.*

FORUMS.DUNGEONDEFENDERS2.COM • 29 JUL 2014

skin milk

V: *skimp milk. Skim milk* gets its name because the milk fat and cream have been *skimmed* off the whole milk. Indeed, when unhomogenized milk settles, it forms a *skin* of cream on top. Skim milk's thinness, which might seem *skimpy,* explains the variant. *Skimp* comes from *scrimp*, but both words are newer than *skim*, a word that may help explain what changed *scrimp* to *skimp*. • *One group drank skin milk 3 times a day and one group didn't eat or drink any dairy, but eat or drank foods that were calcium enriched.*

WWW.SPARKPEOPLE.COM • 29 JUL 2014

slack (your) thirst

Another example in which the modern MALAPROPISM actually resembles the word's original meaning: The term *slake* (quench) derives from the same Middle English word that gives us *slack* (loosen). • *Shasta soda could slack your thirst at 9 cents for a 12-ounce can.*

WWW.ROSSMOORNEWS.COM • 29 JUL 2014

slight of hand

The adjective *slight*—in the sense of a minor or subtle movement of the hand—makes some sense as a description of magic tricks. The noun *sleight*, however, actually means a trick. It derives from a different word, one related to *sly*. • *The conjurer's magazine of secrets in legerdemain & slight of hand.* •

ARCHIVE.ORG • 29 JUL 2014

And our special is a fresh apple cake, with nutmeg, cinnamon, and a caramel frosting . . .

slither of cake

slither of (cake, pie, etc.)

V: *slivered on the ground*. A snake is long and thin, like a *sliver* (a strip) of something, which makes a certain kind of sense—as does the variant, describing the lengthwise motion of a snake. *Slither* derives from the same roots as *slide*, whereas *sliver* comes from a word meaning to split, or divide. • *I sometimes get a tiny slither of pie or maybe a coke that isn't diet. lol.*

WWW.MYFITNESSPAL.COM • 29 JUL 2014

slow gin fizz

V: *slow-eyed*. The *sloe*, or blackthorn, produces a bluish, almond-shaped berry related to the plum, used to flavor *sloe gin*. A *sloe gin fizz* is a cocktail that mixes sloe gin, straight gin, lemon juice, sweetened syrup, and seltzer; the resulting drink fizzes *slowly*. Someone who is *sloe-eyed* has eyes shaped and colored like the berry. • *How do you make a slow gin fizz?*

ANSWERS.YAHOO.COM • 29 JUL 2014

snob (someone) off

Snobs will *snub*—it's seemingly part of the job description—but the words have different origins. *Snob* originally described someone of low social standing (a variant of *cobbler*) who became a social climber and put on airs. The older verb *snub* means to cut something or someone short; on a ship, lines are sometimes *snubbed off*, or shortened. It may also be confused with the expression *put someone off*. • *Try to 'snob' him/her off by not even acknowledging his/her presence!*

TEXTFILES.COM • 29 JUL 2014

soak and wet

V: *soaping wet*. Writers of the EGGCORN may have *soaked and wet* in mind, conflating it with *soaking wet*. The variant confuses *soaping* and *sopping*, both of which occur in bathtubs. • *[M]y iphone got soak and wet. I tried to connect to itunes but the power is showing on and off.*

DISCUSSIONS.APPLE.COM • 30 JUL 2014

soak (your) wild oats

V: *sew (your) wild oats*. Oats require rehydration and cooking before consumption (unless you're a horse), but this uncommon MALAPROPISM doesn't make sense. The variant is more common but similarly incoherent. *Wild oats* are unwanted weeds that sprout when *sown* (planted) in fertile fields, and thus a METAPHOR for a young man's sexual adventures. • *They're so different. brody seems like a playboy, needs time to soak his wild oats.*

WWW.YOUTUBE.COM • 30 JUL 2014

social linguist

Sociolinguistics studies the effects of language on society, and those who do so are *sociolinguists*—except at cocktail parties, when some become *social linguists*. • *As social linguists are fond of saying, "A national language is a dialect with an army."*

WWW.SCRIBD.COM • 30 JUL 2014

soft-peddle

Soft-peddle is mistaken for *soft-selling* (as opposed to more aggressive selling), but the original verb, *soft-pedal*, comes from piano playing, not *peddling*. It means to de-emphasize unpleasant details, as one might use the *pedal* to muffle a piano's loud notes. • *I was told that I had to soft peddle Lutheranism since only about 20% or so of the students were actually Lutheran.*

WWW.ALPB.ORG • 30 JUL 2014

sorted past

V: *sorted relationship*. Mistaken for *sordid*, from the Latin for *dirty*. Keeping names of former lovers organized in a little black book might produce a *sorted past*. Or perhaps, as linguist Arnold Zwicky suggests, it implies a past with many *sorts* of episodes in it (including dirty ones). The variant might be a relationship whose dirty little secrets have been carefully *sorted through*. • *I wasn't troubled by* *his sorted past because the fruit of his present seemed to suggest that he was living a life that was righteous.*

WWW.FACEBOOK.COM • 30 JUL 2014

sort of speak

Confuses *sort of* with *so to speak*, both of which allow a writer to qualify a statement. • *It was sort of speak a form of apprentice time for me to not only learn the things you mentioned, but also to understand how the music business works.*

WWW.69FACESOFROCK.COM • 30 JUL 2014

soul heir

Often a PUN, particularly with regard to musicians. May confuse someone's *soul mate* with his or her *sole heir*, or even a person who inherits the *soul* (the essence) of a person's legacy and inspiration. • *Last week, Cissy Houston and other trustees of Whitney Houston's es-*

soul heir

tate filed a petition to change the structure of payments made to her soul heir. . . .

WWW.FACEBOOK.COM • 30 JUL 2014

Southern draw

Drawl comes from the same root as *draw* and *drag*—it originally meant to loiter and waste time. In America, Southern accents are seen by some as languid and slow, and thus "drawls." A Southern gunslinger might be vulnerable if he says *draw* more slowly than his Yankee counterpart. • *I am new here and would love to meet some ladies with a southern draw.*

WWW.DATEHOOKUP.COM • 30 JUL 2014

spaded (cat, dog, etc.)

v: *spade.* Just as *spades* in a deck of playing cards represent weapons, a spade gets its name from a Latin word for *sword.* The verb meant *to cut,* and historically eunuchs were sometimes referred to as *spades* before *spayed* came to be limited to surgery to neuter female animals. • *Sad news—little Daisy dog was spaded today and it was quite heart wrenching to see her so sad and in a bad way.*

SCILLYDIVERS.BLOGSPOT.COM • 30 JUL 2014

sparkle (a response, a protest, etc.)

May confuse *spark* with *sparkling* (conversation, etc.). *Spark* and *sparkle* are certainly closely related, so the mistake is understandable. However, *spark* conveys the sense of *begin* or *ignite,* whereas something *sparkles* once it has been ignited or light is shined upon it. • *The resolution sparkled an angry response from the pro-lifers.*

FORLIFEANDFAMILY.BLOGSPOT.COM • 30 JUL 2014

spear of influence

Aggression and threats can certainly influence people, so the image of a *spear of influence* makes some sense. A *sphere of influence* may derive from circles drawn by a compass on maps. Shakespeare used *sphere* to describe the part of the world in which a person moved and lived his life—making, of course, a subtle PUN on the surrounding Globe Theatre. • *During 2011, Fount also expanded their spear of influence by providing a la cart services to local indigenous organizations.*

WWW.FOUNTOFMERCY

.COM • 30 JUL 2014

spear of influence

spit and image

v: *spitting image*. Often considered a mistake for *spitting image*, the older *spit and image* also means *an exact double* and is not incorrect, though it's fading from use. *Spitting image* was originally the MALAPROPISM, but it has now replaced *spit and image* as STANDARD USAGE in America. *Spit* has meant *duplicate* since the 1600s, perhaps drawing on the story from Genesis in which God makes Adam in his own image out of dust and breath. This was echoed by Jesus's miracle in the Gospel of John, where he spits into the dust to make mud (Hebrew: *adamah*) with which he restores a blind man's sight. • *She's the spit and image of her mother.*

WWW.FORGOTTENBOOKS.COM • 10 DEC 2014

sprouted (gibberish, nonsense, opinions, etc.)

Unasked-for opinions *sprout* like weeds, and the expression thus makes as much sense as the standard *spout opinions*, and thus is an EGGCORN; the standard phrase derives from *spit*, and possibly *dispute*. Discriminating diners have opinions about *sprouts*—definitely an acquired taste. •

Most likely they will talk a whole bunch and sprout opinions left and right before the baby is born and then it will be the brightest part of their life.

ANSWERS.YAHOO.COM • 31 JUL 2014

spurt of the moment

Confuses getting into *the spirit of the thing* with *the spur of the moment*. The sense of the original, that the moment might *spur* one to act spontaneously, gets rephrased in the EGGCORN to describe a spontaneous outpouring. However, it risks being read as a double entendre. • *In the spurt of the moment i half jokinly proposed he meet me there and to my surprise he wasn't against the idea!*

WWW.EHARMONY.COM • 31 JUL 2014

square quotes

square quotes

Confuses *[square] brackets* with *scare quotes*, the term for using single or double *quotation marks* to emphasize something that has a more fraught meaning (e.g., "Personnel chief to 'visit' local office"). • *[H]e goes straight for the jugular, accusing a coterie of fellow Internet intellectuals for treating what he calls "the Internet"—he uses it in square quotes throughout the book as a fixed entity. . . .*

WWW.AMAZON.COM • 31 JUL 2014

squash (the) subpoena

Quash comes from a Latin word meaning *null* and means to *annul* in a formal legal procedure. The act of *squashing* something flattens it—a less formal procedure but one that can be effective if you throw enough legal weight behind it. • *AOL requested the Virginia court to squash the subpoena but it refused. AOL appealed. Decision, Reversed.*

WWW.SWLEARNING.COM • 31 JUL 2014

squid, damp

A *damp squib* (the British term for a soggy firework) fizzles rather than bangs; *squib* can also refer to a short, fizzling football kick. *Squid* is often the result of a PUN, not a MALAPROPISM, since squids actually prefer dampness. Yet getting a *damp squid* would certainly disappoint someone expecting a bang, so it could be considered an EGGCORN. • *After Spain's rather damp squid of a win over Portugal, to revive our flagging spirits, Chef has made some wonderful Morcilla.*

THEFOODONTHEHILL.TUMBLR.COM • 20 MAY 2014

squirmish

Confuses *squeamish* and *squirmy*, meaning either. Many people are *squeamish* (inclined to nausea) about things that *squirm*. The former is an old word of uncertain origin, and *squirm* is a fairly recent American word that the *OED* says imitates squirmy things. • *ive never got squirmish with my own blood an stuff but jeez i got light headed and went white as a ghost that day!*

WWW.AUSSIEV8.COM.AU • 31 JUL 2014

stalk, laughing

V: *stalk still*. May confuse a plant's *stalk* with a wooden post, or *stock*. A traditional English punishment was imprisonment in a wooden device known as a pillory, or *laughingstock*, where you were ridiculed, pelted with foul items, and sometimes beaten. The variant might suggest someone standing still as a stalking cat. • *Though at first people believed him he was proven wrong and became a laughing stalk of the senate.*

MRGOULDSPAGE.WIKISPACES.COM • 31 JUL 2014

stalk-raving mad

V: *livestalk, star-craving mad, stark raven mad.* An insane person might not only *rave*, as this EGGCORN suggests, he or she could *stalk* around doing crazy things. *Stark raving mad* refers to a naked, mumbling, and shouting lunatic; people suffering psychotic episodes sometimes strip off all their clothes in response to voices in their heads. • *She must have thought i went stalk raving mad when I asked how did that happen?*

WWW.DAILYSTRENGTH.ORG • 31 JUL 2014

statue miles

statue miles

V: *statue of limitations.* Usually just a misspelling. Ancient Roman roads were marked by obelisks every *mile* (measured as a thousand paces by a Roman soldier), and some *statues* and monuments also marked the routes. *Statute miles* were established by law during Elizabethan times and are longer than Roman miles. A *statue of limitations* might regulate how many years after the fact you could be prosecuted for defacing a work of art. • *If the radius of the earth is 3960 regular (statute) miles, how many statue miles are in 1 nautical mile?*

WWW.FREEMATHHELP.COM • 31 JUL 2014

step foot in

The expected phrase is *set foot in*. The *OED* offers plenty of British precedents for *step foot in*, then notes archly that it's "now only U.S." Indeed, it's increasingly common here, though many careful writers consider it an EGG-CORN, since *step foot* seems redundant (what else are you going to step with?). • *Our desire is to reach the group of people that wouldn't step foot in a church, but will sit down and enjoy a beer with us.*

TAMPAUNDERGROUND.COM • 31 JUL 2014

stings attached, no

Usually a PUN or a typo. *No strings attached* often describes uncomplicated deals; *no stings attached* could describe a relationship safe from painful surprises. • *The truth is, we can give with no stings attached because we can trust that our Father in heaven will always provide for us.*

TRACYHURST.COM • 31 JUL 2014

stitch defense, last

The *last stitch* is a knitting term, and someone who *lets out* or *takes out the last stitch* risks everything unraveling. The term gets confused with its HOMOPHONE, *last ditch*, a METAPHOR taken from military trenches. If a last-ditch defense failed, an army's plans could unravel. • *I am a recreational shooter who will use this as a last stitch defense weapon. . . .*

WWW.AR15.COM • 31 JUL 2014

stock, (bean, corn, etc.)

The *stock* of a rifle gets its name from a post or block of wood; some *stalks*, such as asparagus, become very "woody" as they age. Linguists say that in certain dialects of American English, a phenomenon referred to as the *cot/caught merger* exacerbates the confusion by making the words sound the same to some speakers. (*Bean stock*, the soup, is delicious, and isn't a MALAPROPISM at all.) • *This wonderful Royal Bayreuth tray is in absolutely perfect condition depicting Jack looking up the bean stock with a hatchet on one side and a goose laying golden eggs on the other.*

WWW.RUBYLANE.COM • 2 MAY 2014

stocking horse

Perhaps a horse with markings of white *stockings* on its legs. *Stalking horses* were trained to hide gun-bearing hunters who sought to approach game closely. The expression has come to describe something hiding its true purpose. • *Governor Walker is clearly a stocking horse for the far right wing of the Republican Party.*

LAWANDDISORDER.ORG • 26 JUN 2014

stole-away

Many an adventure novel begins with a young protagonist who *steals away* from home, then *stows away* on a ship. So *stole-away* makes some sense. A *stowaway*, however, is "stowed" (placed or stored) as if human cargo, not "stolen." • *He was a stole away on a boat coming to America.*

PREZI.COM • 31 JUL 2014

straddle with

V: *ride side-straddle. Straddle* derives from *stride*, not from a horse's *saddle*, though saddled riders straddle a horse (unless they ride *sidesaddle*). This EGGCORN confuses the METAPHOR of someone's *straddling an issue* (with one foot on either side) and someone *saddled with a problem* (having to bear it on his or her back). • *I didn't want to be straddled with the debt, so we just kept plugging along, doing the best that we could, knowing little but still loving the music.*

WWW.WHATSUP-MAGAZINE.COM • 31 JUL 2014

straight and arrow

V: *strait and arrow, straight and narrow.* Confuses *straight as an arrow* with *the strait and narrow*, and perhaps with the description of someone as *a straight arrow*. In the King James Bible's version of the Gospel of Matthew (7:13-14), Jesus says, "Strait is the gate, and narrow is the way"; strait and narrow mean the same thing. The phrase is often EGGCORN-ized into *the straight and narrow*. • *People need the idea that they are BEING WATCHED, to keep them on the straight and arrow.*

WWW.GODLIKEPRODUCTIONS.COM • 31 JUL 2014

straightjacket

V: *straight-laced. Straightjacket* is now listed by most dictionaries as an acceptable spelling for *straitjacket. Strait* means *confined*, whereas *straight* means *linear*; you could argue that it's an EGGCORN because the confining jacket keeps a disturbed patient safe until he or she is "straight." The variant makes more sense, since someone *straitlaced* (with strict moral attitudes) is likely to be proper and "straight." • *This innovative wine label designed by creative agency Lola Madrid looks like a straightjacket.*

WWW.THENEEDS.COM • 31 JUL 2014

strappings of power

Trappings comes from an Old French word for *drapes*, and medieval *trappings of power* meant decorative finery. Since some of those nobles had subordinates and slaves flogged, there's a certain logic to *strappings*. • *No sooner had they managed to chase away the owner than the pigs turned against the other animals with the strappings of power.*

WWW.STANDARDMEDIA.CO.KE • 31 JUL 2014

strings and arrows

V: *stings and arrows.* Hamlet's "To be, or not to be" soliloquy considers "the *slings and arrows* of outrageous fortune"—the hard and pointy things that life throws at you. *Strings and arrows*, a reference to bowstrings, and the variant, *stings and arrows*, connote pain. • *The UPA Government, with Congress party heading it, is in a state of daze. It seems unable to face the strings and arrows raining on it. . . .*

WWW.HIGHBEAM.COM • 31 JUL 2014

strum up (support, business, etc.)

The *OED* defines *drumming up* as a way of making tea in cans. A better definition might come from medieval times, when itinerant peddlers (*drummers*) announced their arrival with drumbeats to attract business. One could use guitars to solicit support or business, but it

strum up support

wouldn't be as loud. • *But, nevertheless, if you offer competitive prices you'll soon strum up business.*

WWW.SHELL-LIVEWIRE.ORG • 1 AUG 2014

stuff, up to

May confuse *the right stuff* with *up to snuff.* The seventeenth-century English craze for powdered tobacco *snuff*, seen as a stimulant, led to the expression *up to snuff*, meaning clever and sharp. Later it came to mean *up to standard*, or what might be termed having the "right *stuff*." • *I don't have a covered roaster, and I'm not sure that my insulation is really up to stuff.*

CHOWHOUND.CHOW.COM • 31 JUL 2014

suped up

Superman is sometimes informally referred to as "Supes," so by extension a supercharged car could be said to be *suped up.* The *OED* suggests that the standard spelling, *souped up*, may have begun as horseracing cant for injecting a horse with performance-enhancing drugs. But the dictionary also notes the influence of *super*. • *Mobility Scooter With Suped Up Engine Reaches 70 MPH In Snow.*

WWW.8BITBRO.COM • 1 AUG 2014

sword to protect

Usually an autocorrect error where the computer changes the incorrect verb form "swored" (*sworn*) to *sword*; but in some cases—particularly gamer- and fan-fiction—sword-wielding heroes are pledged to protect other characters, and it could be read as an EGGCORN. • *I didn't hate him for lying and stealing and killing the men he was sword to protect.*

WWW.FANFICTION.NET • 1 AUG 2014

synopsis, neural

V: *pleasure synopses*. Confuses *synapses* (junctions) between neurons with *synopses* (brief summaries). One could provide a map that briefly summarized the connections, perhaps—at least those of the brain's pleasure centers. • *It does resemble the neural synopsis and pathways of my inner thoughts.*

WWW.CHARLIEFRANCIS.COM • 1 AUG 2014

t

tackless

A sailboat *in irons* (stalled) might be *tackless*, and the word could mean the opposite of *tacky*. However, this MALAPROPISM is usually just a HOMOPHONE error for *tactless* (lacking sensitivity). • *He was tackless, clumsy, awkward, forgetful, and most of all dense. He lacked all forms of social skills.*

SUGARADDICTEDSHINIGAMI.TUMBLR.COM • 1 AUG 2014

tact

The sailing term *tack* (sailing at an angle toward the wind) is related to *tackle* (nautical ropes and rigging) and is used as a METAPHOR for a course of action. It often gets confused with a *tactic*. Indeed, sailboat racing is often a matter of tactical tacking, or of tacking tactics. • *If you're British, wanting to appear that way, or belong to certain yacht clubs, you'll spell that sailing tact as "gybe."*

WWW.CJR.ORG • 30 JUN 2014

ta-do

Confuses the onomatopoeic *ta-da!* (trumpeting triumph) with *to-do* (commotion), since commotion might announce itself like trumpet sounds. • *Dear Abe, there's currently a lot of ta-do about Anthony Young of the New York Mets losing 18 straight.*

ARTICLES.MCALL.COM • 1 AUG 2014

fairy tail

tail, (fairy, etc.)

V: *old wives' tail, tell-tail, tattle-tail,* etc. May confuse *fairies* with mermaids, who have *tails,* but this is usually just a HOMOPHONE mistake. Some of the variants, however, are more plausible. For instance, a *telltale* on a sailboat is often a string of yarn that shows wind direction, and it can resemble a *tail.* • *The delegation has been told a fairy tail by the Air Force.*

THEWESTERNWORD.COM • 1 AUG 2014

tales of, can't make heads or

The *OED* dates the phrase *heads or tails* (obverse and reverse of a coin) from the late 1600s. An earlier term was *cross and pile,* and ancient Romans called *"capita aut navi"* (*head or ship*). The phrase *can't make heads or tails of* means something that can't be figured out. *Tales* makes some sense here, as if the story can't be discerned. • *Am I the only one who can't make heads or tales of things posted in Twitter?*

WWW.PROMETHEUSFORUM.NE • 1 AUG 2014

tamp down on

Damping down on something means to muffle or restrict it, *suppressing* its fire, as with a damper. To *tamp down on* something would pack it more tightly, actually making it more concentrated and intense; the mistake has an EGGCORN-ish logic nevertheless. • *Even lack of sleep couldn't tamp down his excitement once he launched into the intricacies of the cases. . . .*

TODAY.DUKE.EDU • 2 AUG 2014

tarter sauce

Some sauces are *tarter*, some are sweeter, but few are made with *cream of tartar* (potassium hydrogen tartrate). *Tartar sauce* gets its name from the French *sauce tartare* (named after the fierce Asian Tartars for its tangy taste). Its main ingredients are mayonnaise and mustard. • *Pond raised catfish, blackend with tarter sauce is a favorite in our part of the country.*

WWW.HOUSEBOATMAGAZINE.COM • 2 AUG 2014

taught muscles

The phenomenon of muscle memory suggests that muscles must be *taught* the proper actions, but *taut* (or tense) muscles are not required. Indeed, relaxed muscles are often the goal. • *My stomach and chest were tight and my muscles were so taught that I thought I was having a heart attack.*

TREESING98042.BLOGSPOT.COM • 2 AUG 2014

teatotaller

Mistaken for *teetotaler* (abstainer). *Tea* was certainly on the beverage menu for teetotalers but wasn't the source of the name. It was imposed on members of the British Total Abstinence Society much as we might say a "Capital-T Totaler." • *But compared to most of the people at the Astor Center I was a teatotaller.*

NRNFOODWRITER.BLOGSPOT.COM • 2 AUG 2014

Momm . . . !

KEEP OUT

THIS MEANS YOU

scarlet teenager

Teenager, (Scarlet, Summer) Rare, and usually a PUN. A *scarlet teenager* might be one whose mother catches him reading *Playboy*. The *Scarlet Tanager* and *Summer Tanager* are colorful birds whose names derive from *Tangara*, a word from the language of the Tupi people of Brazil. • *Beautiful Watercolor painting of Scarlet Teenager bird Signed!*

WWW.EBAY.IE • 2 AUG 2014

tenant of, basic

V: *main tent, basic tent*, etc. *Tenet* and *tenant* come from the same Latin root—*tenere* (*to hold*); *tent* comes from *tendĕre* (*to stretch*). A *tenet* is a belief or principle that one holds, and a *tenant* is someone who holds property. • *The basic tenant of the Scientific Method is that you can only disprove, you can never prove anything scientifically.*

FOG.CCSF.CC.CA.US • 3 MAY 2014

tenderbox

According to the U.S. Treasury, the dollar bill is "legal *tender* [a lawful medium of exchange] for all debts, public and private," so a cash register could be called a *tender box*. Unless you have money to burn, however, you aren't likely to confuse it with a *tinderbox*, in which dry material used to start fires is kept. • *Unfortunately, as the summer sun grows hotter and the days drier, those waist high grasses will become an explosive tender box....*

WWW.LOBOWATCH.ORG • 2 AUG 2014

tender hooks, on

Tenterhooks were originally used to stretch canvas for *tents*, but they also came to describe hooks in general, including those on which meat was hung to cure and *tenderize*. • *Last Monday night, the wrestling world was on tender hooks. Not for a very long time had an episode of Monday Night Raw been so eagerly anticipated....*

BLEACHERREPORT.COM • 26 SEPT 2014

ten-yeared professor

V: *ten-year track position*, *tenure tract*. It usually takes four to six years for a published junior professor to get academic *tenure*. *Tenure,* from the Old French *to hold*, helps guarantee academic freedom and job security. A scholarly publication might be termed a *tenure tract*. • *He is a "ten-yeared" professor. He can almost say anything and not get fired.*

WWW.RATEMYPROFESSORS.COM • 4 AUG 2014

term of phrase

A *term* and a *phrase* both describe word usage, so this makes some sense. A *turn of phrase*, however, means that one fashions a *phrase* the way one might fashion a piece of wood *turned* on a lathe—it conveys the sense of crafting the phrase. The *OED*'s first example of someone's turning the phrase *turn of phrase* is Ben Franklin, in 1779. • *What a nice term of phrase for people who do things differently to you. Whatever happened to live and let live?*

WWW.MYFITNESSPAL.COM • 4 AUG 2014

the rears, rent is in

Confuses *behind in the rent* with *the rent is in arrears* (owed). Or perhaps a person who pays his bill with hams. • *No, a landlord can not grant the Police permission to enter a rented room, even if the rent is in the rears, without a warrant.*

FREEPATRIOT.ORG • 23 JUL 2014

the skies, blessing in

Confuses an unexpected celestial blessing, such as the rainbow that God revealed to Noah in Genesis, with the common phrase *blessing in disguise*. The original has been attributed to the Reverend James Hervey, a very popular devotional writer of mid-eighteenth-century England. • *I guess my allergic reaction was a blessing in the skies after all.*

CHRONICLESOFANADVENTURISTA

.BLOGSPOT.COM • 6 MAY 2014

hammer and thongs

thongs, go at it hammer and

Hammer and thongs suggests kinky sex or carpentry in flip-flops rather than the clanging blacksmith's shop METAPHOR of the STANDARD USAGE, *go at it hammer and tongs*. The usual phrase connotes vehemence or energy. • *It was a pretty uneventful second half although both teams went at it hammer and thongs in this titanic battle.*

WATERFORDWOLVES.COM • 4 AUG 2014

through me for a loop

The original phrase was *knocked (me) for a loop* and appears to refer to boxing. Wrestling, with its throws, probably produced *threw (me) for a loop*. However, since loops are open in the middle and one could be thrown *through* them, this qualifies as an EGGCORN about getting all tangled up. • *I love graphic novels and the parts where it seemed like she was in my head really through me for a loop.*

FORUMS.PSYCHCENTRAL.COM • 4 AUG 2014

throws, death

V: *throws of passion, throngs of passion. Death throes,* from Old English words for *calamity* and *suffering,* implies the suffering of death, not fatal Judo or wrestling *throws* (from an Old English word for *twist*). The use of *throw* to describe amorous grappling might qualify as an EGGCORN, however. • *In its death throws, the core of a star like Lucy or our own Sun becomes exposed and slowly cools down over time.*

WWW.SPACETODAY.ORG • 4 AUG 2014

tick in (your) eye

A *tick* (a parasitic arachnid of the suborder *Ixodida*) can attach itself in or near one's eye, which might indeed cause one to blink uncontrollably. The usual word is *tic*, from the French phrase *tic douloureux*, used to describe a facial twitch. Its origin is uncertain, but has nothing to do with blood-sucking bugs. The example cited, from a collection of MONDEGREENS, is also an EGGCORN. • *He's got a tick in her eye. Actual lyric: She's got a ticket to ride. (Beatles).*

WWW.CORSINET.COM • 4 NOV 2014

tidy-whitey

V: *tidy–widy.* Briefs (or *tighty whiteys*) certainly look trim on underwear models, so *tidy whitey* qualifies as an EGGCORN. They are also available in *wide* sizes. • *I finally watched the first episode of Breaking Bad. It was basically just some old guy dancing around in his tidy whiteys.*

NEW.SPRING.ME • 4 AUG 2014

time (you) over

V: *tie (you) over.* Inbound current can *tide* a deep-hulled boat *over* a harbor bar, helping one "get by." But the phrase is also used in the sense that one has enough of something to survive for a while, which gets confused with *the time being.* Or it could refer to involuntary restraint. • *Qantas served tasty dinners with complementary good Western Au wine, a lovely hot breakfast and a bag of snacks to time me over in between.*

WWW.TRAVELBLOG.ORG • 16 AUG 2014

toe-headed child

toe-headed child

Few people spin flax from *tow* (bundles of flax fibers) anymore, so the expression *tow-headed child* (to describe a child's pale blond hair) may not make much sense. The confusion comes from a bald baby, or a child with short blond hair, which might resemble a pale *toe* to some. • *Then I got scared because I was expecting a toe-headed child and I didn't know what to do about a red-head.*

WWW.THEHIPMOTHERSHIP.COM • 4 AUG 2014

tolled, all

V: *all total, untolled.* Confuses *toll* (a fee charged), the standard *all told* (totaled), and told's HOMOPHONE *tolled* (ringing of bells), as if the bells had concluded ringing up a sale. • *All tolled, these five buyers captured $800 million in multi-family real estate and represent 54% of the total marketplace.*

all tolled

WWW.COLLIERSCANADA.COM • 14 MAR 2014

tooth and throat singing

Rare. *Tuva,* a republic in south-central Russia near Mongolia, is famous for wordless chanting called *throat singing.* It employs overtones (harmonics on a fundamental note) so that the singer seems to be singing several notes at once. • *The new ensemble wanted to explore untraditional vocal techniques and was focusing on tooth and throat singing, yodeling and belting, all of which found their way into "Partita."*

WWW.CHRON.COM • 4 AUG 2014

top seed, grow like

Grow like Topsy comes from *Uncle Tom's Cabin,* in which the slave girl Topsy, asked where she comes from, famously says, "I spect I grow'd. Don't think nobody never made me." It was once a byword for something growing wild. The EGGCORN *grow like top seed* confuses the expression

grow like top seed

with *topsoil* and *seeds* of top quality. • *My legislation is intended to be a form of property tax relief, by setting a specific monetary cap on legal fees so they do not grow and grow like top seed.*

WWW.ANCHORRISING .COM • 11 JUN 2014

torchpaper

Touchpaper, impregnated with niter, is used to set off explosives and is a METAPHOR for something likely to ignite (or *touch off*) a dispute. *Torchpaper* is a natural mistake. • *I was holding a piece of burning torch-paper in my hand, while Harry Johnson was letting the powder from the flask fall on the end of the paper[.]*

WWW.SAXONLODGE.NET • 4 AUG 2014

tow the line

tow the line

A common EGG-CORN, as the expression means *shape up,* and many writers confuse it with *pull (tow) your own weight. Toe the line* comes from British naval tradition, where sailors lined up (toes to the line) for inspection to make sure they were sober and ready to perform their duties. • *Corporations suing governments who don't tow the line.*

WWW.DORSETEYE.COM • 4 AUG 2014

tracks of land

V: *track houses*. Easily confused HOMOPHONES, *track* and *tract* have closely parallel word histories. A *tract* (related to *tractor*) was land marked by dragging boundary lines, and a *track* was the line left by the dragging. Today, *tract* describes the land, and *track* the roads or paths on it. • *The Municipality is endowed with vast track of land which could be developed agricutural and estate purposes.*

WWW.GHANADISTRICTS.COM • 4 AUG 2014

tract lighting

The *tracts* of land on which tract houses (nearly identical houses in a suburban development) are built would logically be illuminated by *tract lighting*—but *track lighting* would be what's on electrified metal tracks on ceilings inside the houses. • *I am trying to install a tract lighting in my kitchen—i have an outlet that is on the wall close to the ceiling[.]*

WWW.DOITYOURSELF.COM • 4 AUG 2014

trader

V: *traderous*. Many a *traitor* has been a *trader* in state secrets. Although the two HOMOPHONES aren't synonymous, there's enough overlap to lead to some EGGCORNS. • *But does this sentiment make her a trader to the cause of women's liberation?*

LADYBERD.COM • 4 AUG 2014

trades, genetic

V: *inherited trade*. Many a science fiction novel has been written about the *trade in human genetic qualities* such as good looks, intelligence, and long life. Now, though, manipulating *genetic traits* in living creatures isn't just fiction. • *Several experts come to the conclusion that while some people may have a predisposition in their genetic trades for violence or cancer. . . .*

WWW.CHOOPERSGUIDE.COM • 4 AUG 2014

traits, jack of all

A *Jack of all trades* has long been the name given to a handyman able to do anything passably; *traits*, however, are individual characteristics. The EGGCORN may confuse it with card games in which jacks are wild. • *I started out as a youth director, and now I am that and a jack of all traits.*

WWW.ROYALPIN.COM • 4 AUG 2014

trite and true

Often an ironic PUN, as even worn-out ideas can have some truth to them. The phrase confuses the adjective *trite* (from the Latin for *rubbed*, or *worn*) with the adjective *tried* (originally meaning separated, as grain is sifted) in the expression *tried and true* (well-tested and reliable). • *Krystal tells us he means that "genre" novels "stick to the trite-and-true, relying on stock characters . . ."*

JUNEGILLAM.COM • 5 AUG 2014

turban, (steam, gas, wind, etc.)

A *turban* is wrapped around the head, and a *turbine* spins to produce power. The headdress's name comes from Persian words, and the machine's name comes from the Latin *turbo* (*whirlwind*). Both go around, and the words sound alike. • *Power is supplied by battery charged by solar panels, or wind turban or generator.*

wind turban

WWW.KEMMERERHOMES.COM •

5 AUG 2014

turns with, come to

Often expresses a reversal of direction instead of *come to terms with*, where the METAPHOR is that of a contract. • *It's like a metaphor for letting go, and when I walked around there were a lot of people meditating and trying to come to turns with events in their lives.*

HOTCAKES.INFO • 17 MAY 2014

u

ultraviolent light

Light in the *ultraviolet* (UV) spectrum can damage—*do violence to*, you might say—living cells such as those in human skin. *Violet* and *violent*, though close in spelling, don't share word histories aside from the fact that

ultraviolent light

both come from classical Latin. • *Go green with this environmentally friendly liquid laminate that is bonded and cured with ultraviolent light.*

WWW.TRIO-SOLUTIONS.COM • 8 AUG 2014

unchartered territory

Charter and *chart* have the same origin—the Latin for *paper*—but a charter is a grant of rights, and a chart is a sheet of visual information such as a map or diagram. *Uncharted territory*, since it hadn't been mapped or parceled out, was typically *unchartered,* too. • *He loves asking us to walk on water. He takes pride in calling us into unchartered territory.*

CHRYSTALEVANSHURST.COM • 5 AUG 2014

underline problem

V: *underlining problem.* The EGGCORN suggests a problem so significant that it is *underlined,* as opposed to a hidden, or *underlying* problem. • *We are helping you solve the underline problem: why are you AFRAID to announce your pregnancy?*

COMMUNITY.BABYCENTER.COM • 5 AUG 2014

undo influence

Confuses the verb *undo* (unfasten or cancel) and the adjective *undue* (inappropriate). You could argue that *don't* (do not) is the un-*do.* So *undo influence* might be an EGGCORN for *negative influence.* • *It's also possible that one or two key staff have some kind of hangup about it and are exercising undo influence in this situation.*

DISABILITYTHINKING.BLOGSPOT.COM • 5 AUG 2014

unphased

V: *phased. Faze* comes from an Old English word meaning

to *frighten off*, but as with many other plain Anglo-Saxon words, modern writers try to dress it up. The Greek-influenced *ph* spelling for *f* seems to be a way of doing this. Spelling it *phase* is not really even an EGGCORN, as the sense of *phase* rarely *phits*. • *He was completely un-phased as a three year old and has just got on with life.*

WWW.CAYBERRYDARTMOORS.CO.UK • 5 AUG 2014

un-suite

French inns don't advertise rooms with bathrooms *en suite*; the French term is *avec salle de bains attenante*. *En suite* actually means *in sequence* and originally referred to two rooms in sequence that became known as a *suite* in hospitality lingo. In English, rooms *en suite* came to mean rooms with attached bathrooms. • *The Presidents room is one of our more luxurious rooms also with seaview, aircon, barfridge and the un-suite bathroom with spa bath and double shower and tv*[.]

WWW.SLEEPING-OUT.CO.ZA • 5 AUG 2014

untracked, can't get

Confuses *can't get unstuck* with *can't get on track*. *Can't get on track* is a METAPHOR for train derailment; the train needs to get back on track. *Can't get unstuck* suggests someone *bogged down* in a mire. *Untracked* might be an EGGCORN in the sense of someone's wanting to change direction when stuck on an established track. • *Women's basketball team can't get untracked at Saddleback*[.]

IRVINEVALLEY.PRESTOSPORTS.COM • 6 AUG 2014

unvaluable

Literally of no value. But the EGGCORN confuses *invaluable* (priceless) with adjectives such as *unmatched* and *unrivaled* when describing something that one is unable to put a value on. • *God bless you all for such an unvaluable contribution to humanity and to make this world a worth and happy place to live in.*

ROTAPLAST.TYPEPAD.COM • 6 AUG 2014

uphauled by

V: *uphauled at, uphauling.* To *appall* someone is to dismay them. *Appall* derives from a Middle English word meaning *grow pale*, whereas *haul* comes from antique French and means *to pull*. It might be confused with expressions such as *bring up short* or *upset*. • *I was uphauled by her remarks and I couldn't understand why you wouldn't want your child to do better?*

KELSEYHOOKS-MYINTERNSHIPBLOG.BLOGSPOT.COM • 6 AUG 2014

upmost extent

V: *upmost effort. Utmost* (or *uttermost*) actually means *outermost,* so the *utmost extent* would mark the outer limits of something. This EGGCORN confuses it with *uppermost* (as in *uppermost in one's mind*—most conscious in one's mind). • *The goal is not only to present a product online, but also to duplicate the touch and feel of the product to the upmost extent.*

SEGOMA.COM • 6 AUG 2014

veil of tears

Burma-Shave, a shaving cream company, once had signs that reminded us that "Within this vale/ of toil and sin/ your head grows bald/ but not your chin," from Cervantes's observation that life is a *vale* (valley) *of tears* (inspired by the "valley of the shadow of death" of Psalm 23). But a *veil of tears* makes sense, too—the way tears make it hard for you to see, and how life's woes *veil* your sight with weeping. • *We live in a veil of tears, in the valley of the shadow of death.*

WWW.HOPE-AURORA.ORG • 6 AUG 2014

very close veins

Usually a literary MALAPROPISM used for comic effect to describe the medical condition *varicose veins*. There's little evidence to be found on the Internet that people actually make the mistake—mostly versions of the same (apparently apocryphal) account of a mother's excuse for her child's school absence due to "very close veins." • *[Louis] Armstrong had been suffering from varicose veins (which he called "very close veins") since at least 1964. It turned into phlebitis. . . .*

BOOKS.GOOGLE.COM • 16 APR 2014

view, to name a

May confuse *to name a few* with IDIOMS such as *in my view* and *from that point of view*. It could be an EGGCORN when used to describe examples—particularly examples of places. • *Ortler, Bernina, Weildspitze, Weißkugel, Hintere Schwärze, Similaun, just to name a view summits you can see.*

WWW.EVERYTRAIL.COM • 6 AUG 2014

vintage point

vintage point

Usually just a misspelling—*vintage* (old like fine wine) for *vantage* (a place from which one can see things). It could also be a simple MALAPROPISM, unless it refers to a spot overlooking, say, California's Napa Valley. Aside from PUNS, few examples can be found that convey the sense of a *fine* or *old* viewpoint. • *This trip emphasizes all of these with sightseeing from the vintage point of the saddle while creating a great excuse to eat.*

WWW.TRIPS2LEARN.COM • 6 AUG 2014

voiceterous

A rowdy crowd is often characterized as *boisterous* (from a Middle English word for *rustic and coarse*), so the EGG-CORN *voiceterous* seems natural. It may confuse *vocal* with *boisterous*. • *Some crowds in Toronto are really rabid. Philly always brings a very voiceterous crowd, too.*

WWW.GTX0.COM • 6 AUG 2014

wail away at

V: *wale away at*. The American expression *whale away at* (strike, beat) is of uncertain origin, according to the *OED*, which speculates that it might come from thrashing with a *whalebone* whip. *Wale* is a much older verb, and it means to mark the flesh with *wales* (weals); perhaps *whale* conflates *wale* and *whip*; both prompt *wails*. • *Our hitters will never stand at the plate and just mindlessly wail away at pitch after pitch.*

JUGSSPORTS.COM • 6 AUG 2014

want, as is (your)

Confuses *want* (desire) and *wont* (habit). The sense of the standard phrase is *as you're used to doing,* and the MALA-PROPISM's is *as you wish to do.* • *I was on a train with my earphones shoved in my ears completely ignoring my fellow commuters (as is my want early in the morning). . . .*

WWW.SUNRISEGROUP.ORG • 6 AUG 2014

want for (your) arrest

Police radio jargon sometimes includes the phrase *wants and warrants,* which is shorthand for *Is the person wanted for anything?* and *Are there any warrants for the person's arrest?* This EGGCORN confuses the two. • *The bank has no power to issue a want for your arrest.*

WWW.AVVO.COM • 6 AUG 2014

war mongrel

V: *power mongrel*. Shakespeare's Mark Anthony famously declaims, "Cry 'Havoc!' and let slip the dogs of war," and this MALAPROPISM would seem to follow suit, confusing *mongrel* (a dog of mixed breed) with *monger* (a dealer or promoter). Perhaps some *warmongers* pursue their goals doggedly. • *Did anyone call Saddam Hessian a war mongrel?? This man who killed millions and started the attack that brought on the war[.]*

LUVLYDOLL.TUMBLR.COM • 6 AUG 2014

wasteband

wasteband

People generally tie up their garbage bags with a *waste band* and their pants with a *waistband*—an EGGCORN, perhaps, in the case of disposable undergarments. • *SureCare Slip On Undergarments have a one piece elastic wasteband that combines easy, slip on convenience with a snug, comfortable fit.*

WWW.DHPHOMEDELIVERY.COM • 6 AUG 2014

parting of the waves

waves, parting of the

An EGGCORN of biblical proportions. When the Israelites crossed the Red Sea, the *parting of the waters* marked a *parting of the ways* with their Egyptian masters. "The parting of the way" comes from the King James Bible (Ezekiel 21:21) and may also be confused with Jesus's *calming of the waves* (Mark 4:35). • *The parting of the waves came just over two furlongs out, when Quarter Moon poached what appeared to be a decisive advantage.*

WWW.INDEPENDENT.CO.UK • 26 SEPT 2014

way in

To *weigh in* means to lend your *weight* or influence to a discussion, problem, or dispute. It means imposing yourself, and in that sense finding a *way in* to the problem makes some sense. • *It is my turn to way in on this mystery.*

DISTRACTION-138.TUMBLR.COM • 6 AUG 2014

weigh-lay

V: *weigh-station, by the weigh-side.* Highway robbers would typically *waylay* (lie in ambush for) their victims, though the word today mostly just means to interrupt someone. The MALAPROPISM may confuse *waylay* with *weigh in*, in the sense of interrupting with one's opinion. The variants for *waystation* and *wayside* could apply to truck scales along a freeway. • *Ironically, I too was weigh laid today by a bird watcher.*

SOMMERLOVINBLOG.WORDPRESS.COM • 8 AUG 2014

well-healed

Heel was an old synonym for *spur*. *Well-heeled* originally meant well-armed, inspired perhaps by the heels (spurs) of fighting gamecocks, and came to mean well-equipped with money. The MALAPROPISM might be an EGGCORN that suggests the ability of money to make up for, or *heal*, many deficiencies. • *It is a fascinating place full of rather well healed tourists, once again we fit in so well. . . . not!*

NBTHEMANLYFERRY.BLOGSPOT.COM • 8 AUG 2014

wet your appetite

Confuses *wet your whistle* (drink) with *whet your appetite* (stimulate your hunger). *Wetting* your appetite, however, would dampen it, not *whet* (sharpen) it. • *Fly Cargo comes to BlackBerry 10 and with a free version to wet your appetite.*

wet your appetite

CRACKBERRY.COM • 8 AUG 2014

wheedle down

Confuses *wheedle* (beg, or coax) with *wheel-and-deal* (haggle). • *I think the seller is convinced I am a thief who is going to try to wheedle them down on price and then make a false insurance claim.*

HUGHHOLLOWELL.ORG • 8 AUG 2014

wheelbarrel

A *wheelbarrow* gets its name from a wheeled version of a stretcher on which cargo or human bodies were carried, known as a *barrow,* or *bier.* A *barrel* can be used to carry things too, and barrels, like *wheels*, will roll, adding to

wheelbarrel

the confusion. • *Are those the little itty bitty wheels that be-*
long on a wheelbarrel?

WWW.ADVRIDER.COM • 8 AUG 2014

whenst (you) came

Whence is already an antique word that dates from Middle
English, and the EGGCORN further antiquates it by adding the *-st* of *whilst*. • *Entities, Demons and Devils return*
from whenst you came, never to return to us, our reality or
our bodies ever again.

WWW.ORGONEENERGY.ORG • 8 AUG 2014

whoa is me!

V: *the whoas of, woeth me, woe as me.* Examples of the poetic
interjection of remorse *Woe is me!* date from Old and
Middle English, and it is often translated that way
from the Bible's book of Job (10:15). *Whoa!*, on the
other hand, means *stop* and is an informal expression of
surprise deriving from an equestrian command ("I'm
like, 'whoa!'"). Sometimes just a misspelling, sometimes an EGGCORN that confuses the two uses. • *Now,*
I'm saying 'whoa is me', all the things I should've done dif-
ferently.

RACHELYHARRIS.BLOGSPOT.COM • 8 AUG 2014

wholemark

The Hall of Goldsmiths in England stamped gold with its
mark to certify authenticity and purity, and a *hall-mark*
or *hallmark*, like a signature, has come to be a byword
for and measure of the quality of something. *Wholeness*
is also associated with quality, so *wholemark* probably
qualifies as an EGGCORN. • *We only use straight line tea from*

highland estates to guarantee exquisite flavour, quality, freshness and full bodied which is wholemark of Pure Ceylon Tea.

SERENDIB-TEA.ORG • 8 AUG 2014

whole-scale

Confuses *wholesale* and *large-scale*, or *on a massive scale. Wholesale* connotes large lots of goods for sale, so the confusion makes some sense. • *This sort of whole-scale theft and fraud merits more than passing mention.*

WWW.CITY-JOURNAL.ORG • 26 SEPT 2014

whorefrost

Usually a PUN or typo, but perhaps sometimes a characterization of a *killing frost* as something deplorable. *Hoar* (gray, old) and *whore* (harlot, prostitute) don't share an ETYMOLOGY; the latter comes from old Germanic words for "adulterer." • *[T]oday we have ice fog and its beautiful with the trees all covered with whorefrost.*

ARCHIVES1.TWOPLUSTWO.COM • 8 AUG 2014

wild, worth (your)

V: *worthwild.* Often a PUN. *While* involves time and *worth (your) while* means something worth spending time on; arguably, you could also seek something worth pouring your untamed (*wild*) energies into. • *I decided if I could do it cheap enough then it was worth my wild to give it a go!*

WWW.HAMMOCKFORUMS.NET • 9 AUG 2014

wild awake

People suffering from insomnia often report a feeling of *wildness* or panic at their inability to sleep, which may help explain this EGGCORN. It may also confuse *wild-eyed* with *wide-eyed*, which might characterize someone who is *wide awake* in the middle of the night. • *Another time I was watching TV on my couch lying down, wasn't even trying to sleep I was wild awake.*

FORUMS.CLUBRSX.COM • 8 AUG 2014

wildflowers, spread like

Wildflowers can indeed *spread* quickly (just ask those with dandelions in their lawns), but not as fast as *wildfire*. Wildfires are actually a key mechanism in nature for spreading wildflowers, as scorched earth and denuded trees allow new plants to grow. • *It spread like wildflowers, people were randomly prepaying for hundreds of Timmys special brew . . . annonomously.*

ONYXBARBERS.COM • 9 AUG 2014

willow-the-wisp

Will-o'-the-wisp and *jack-o'-lantern* name the same phenomenon of mysterious lights that lure travelers into bogs and marshes in European folklore and fairy lore. J.R.R. Tolkien's character Old Man Willow and the Harry Potter books' Whomping Willow attest that *willow* trees (genus *Salix*) are also associated with magic, spirits, and gates to the underworld. *Will* is a generic name for a person (supposedly one cursed to wander the marshes) and has no connection to the tree. • *A few moments later, he saw a willow-the-wisp. Soon, it exploded in a flash of light.*

SCROLLSTUDIO.COM • 9 AUG 2014

wind-nut

wind-nut

v: *right wind*, *left wind*. A *wing-nut*, with two aerodynamic-looking *wings* for tightening, might be confused with a *wind-vane*, and metaphorically with "hot air" in its political sense • *Because in hondas infinate wisdom they use a wind nut on the belt tensioner.*

WWW.GARAGEJOURNAL.COM • 9 AUG 2014

windowseal

Windowsills, properly made, *seal* out water, so this is certainly an EGGCORN. *Sill* comes from the Old English word for a wooden foundation, and *seal* from the Latin word for a mark of ownership. • *I have tried using a spray bottle with water, raising the blinds so [my cat] can sit on the window seal, and also spanking her.. she seems to enjoy the water, and isn't interested in sitting in the window.*

WWW.ASK.COM • 4 AUG 2014

winfall

Confuses a *windfall* with a *win*—and possibly with a *win-win proposition*. A *windfall*, which gets its name from fruit that drops from trees without having to be picked, connotes unexpected good fortune or profits. • *A company like a siemens or GE might just snap them up for a couple of bucks/share. Chump change for them a winfall for us!*

INVESTORSHUB.ADVFN.COM • 9 AUG 2014

wink and a prayer, on a

v: *On a whim and a prayer.* Confuses *a wink and a nod* with the song "Comin' In on a Wing and a Prayer." The lyrics, written during World War II by Harold Adamson, told of a bomber pilot returning to base with one engine disabled and only the wing functioning. *A wink and a nod* connotes unspoken understanding. The variant suggests trusting to luck.

on a wink and a prayer

• *She quit her full time position as Manager with a local restaurant after 19 years and started with me with a wink and a prayer.*

WWW.DLEANCHOICEFIT.COM • 9 AUG 2014

wise tale, old

V: *old wives' tail.* A wonderful example of an EGGCORN: so-called *old wives' tales,* not based on formal learning, are often cited as examples of unlettered *wisdom.* The variant makes less sense, as a *tail* has little to do with telling tales. • *So I kept hearing about Geritol but I thought it was an old wise tale.*

COMMUNITY.BABYCENTER.COM • 9 AUG 2014

wonderlust

Wonder and *wander* get mixed up often, but the idea of *wonderlust*—the desire to see the wonders of the world—is a particularly appealing EGGCORN that may confuse Lewis Carroll's *Wonderland* with the old German notion of *wanderlust*. *Wanderlust* is first recorded in English in the early 1900s and describes the urge to hit the road in search of adventure. • *I both have a nerdy and jock side to me and still have a bit of wonderlust in me (I like to travel and explore).*

WWW.MATCH.COM • 9 AUG 2014

wrangled (an invitation, ticket, etc.)

No one knows exactly how *wangle* originated, but it was nineteenth-century printers' SLANG that meant getting something by persuasion. *Wrangle*, on the other hand, comes from *wrestling*, and one of its meanings is to bargain for something. • *She just wrangled an invitation on her phone, using insider back channel voodoo, in minutes*[.]

JASMINEEMILYLIFE.TUMBLR.COM • 9 AUG 2014

wrapped attention

Rapt is an older version of *rapture*, and *rapt attention* means someone paying attention as if *enraptured*. But one might also describe that person metaphorically as *wrapped up* in whatever occupied his attention. *Wrapped* historically means enfolded in cloth or a similar wrapping. • *Both the students and the teachers listened with wrapped attention to these stories.*

WWW.AUROVILLE.ORG • 9 AUG 2014

wreck havoc

V: *reek havoc*. The difference between *wreaking* and *wrecking* is not only a long *ē*; they differ also by definition: doing something on purpose instead of doing it by accident. *Wreak* and *wreck* actually share an ETYMOLOGY, going back to a Scandinavian word meaning *drive*. *Wreck* conveys the sense of a ship driven onto rocks. *Wreaking havoc* (destruction), meanwhile, suggests driving vengeance upon others. • *After high school, Dave attended Allegheny College where he wrecked havoc on this cute college town for four years.*

WWW.WEDDINGWIRE.COM • 9 AUG 2014

wreckless driving

A common error, usually just a simple spelling goof or HOMOPHONE-based MALAPROPISM, that confuses *reckless driving* (driving without *reckoning*, or heed) with the *wrecks* it causes. Literally, *wreckless* would mean *without a wreck*. • *Los Angeles Dodgers outfielder Yasiel Puig was arrested for wreckless driving in Collier County Florida. . . .*

WWW.THOUGHTSOFAJEANIUS.COM • 9 AUG 2014

wringer, dead

V: *wring the changes, put through the ringer.* The origin of *dead ringer*, American SLANG meaning a near-double, is obscure. English bell-ringing teams sometimes brought in substitute *ringers* for change-ringing, but the activity was never very popular in the US; it may be a horse-racing term. A *dead wringer* might be a deceased laundry worker, but otherwise it's probably just a HOMOPHONE error. • *Well I'm a dead wringer for matthew mcconaughey in 'two for the money' ha.*

INVESTORSHUB.ADVFN.COM • 9 AUG 2014

x, y, z

play it by year

year, play it by

Conflates the musical term *play it by ear* (without written music or instructions) with such IDI-OMS as *by the year* or *year by year*. Often just a typo. *Playing it by year* might suggest "taking your time." • *I don't imagine there will be much sleep going on Wed night! Why don't we play it by year then.*

WWW.SPLITCOASTSTAMPERS.COM •
9 AUG 2014

youthamism

You could argue that *youthamism* is a new coinage for *youthful* SLANG *for obscene words,* but most of the examples that Google turns up seem to be honest mistakes. Still, many are in the context of youth culture, so this certainly qualifies as an EGGCORN for *euphemism* (a mild word substituted for something vulgar). • *That isn't a youthamism we promise, but there will be occasions where guards use the talents of the prison population for their own ends.*

WWW.GAMERZINES.COM • 9 AUG 2014